305.8
F   Franklin, Paula An-
              gle

              Melting pot or
              not?

DUE DATE

DISCARD

MELTING POT OR NOT?

Debating Cultural Identity

Paula A. Franklin

—Multicultural Issues—

ENSLOW PUBLISHERS, INC.

44 Fadem Road	P.O. Box 38
Box 699	Aldershot
Springfield, N.J. 07081	Hants GU12 6BP
U.S.A.	U.K.

Library of Congress Cataloging-in-Publication Data

Franklin, Paula Angle, 1928-
    Melting Pot or Not? Debating Cultural Identity / Paula A. Franklin.
        p. cm.— (Multicultural Issues)
    Includes bibliographical references and index.
    ISBN 0-89490-644-5
    1. United States—Ethnic relations—Juvenile literature. 2. United States—Race
relations—Juvenile literature. 3. Ethnicity—United States—Juvenile literature.
4. Group identity—United States—Juvenile literature. I. Title II. Series.
E184.A1F67 1995
305.8'00973—dc20   94-37945
                                                        CIP
                                                        AC

Printed in the United States of America

10 9 8 7 6 5 4 3 2 1

Illustration Credits: *American History Illustrated,* p. 24; AP/Wide World Photos, p.
54; Cumberland County Historical Society, pp. 81, 82; *Harper's New Monthly
Magazine,* p. 71; *Illustrated London News,* p. 47; Katherine McGlynn, p. 17; Mary
Bloom, p. 62; Sallon McElligot Agency, p. 96; Stephenie Hollyman, p. 6; United
States Department of Commerce, p. 88; UPI/Bettmann, p. 37.

Cover Illustration: Enslow Publishers, Inc.

Contents

How Do You Say *Assembly* in Cantonese?

Teenagers clatter up and down the stairs. Lockers bang open and shut. Teachers write on chalkboards: math problems to compute, dates to know, and vocabulary to learn.

In many ways Seward Park High School in New York City is just like other high schools in the United States. Students worry about grades, plan for college, root for the school teams, and lead a busy social life. In some ways the school is special. Every morning, after the Pledge of Allegiance, announcements over the public address system are made in three languages—English, Spanish, and Cantonese (a Chinese language). Roughly four out of five students at Seward Park High School come from homes in which English is not the main language spoken.[1] In these families, the parents were not born in the United States. Neither were many of their children. The New York City Board of Education sums up the high school's population this way: 46 percent Hispanic,

Seward Park High School's diversity is suggested in this informal conference involving a teacher and two of his students. The student on the left is African American, the student on the right is Hispanic, and the teacher is Jewish.

38 percent Asian, 14 percent black, and 2 percent white. (There are also a few Native Americans, who total far less than 1 percent.)

Seward Park High School is in a part of southern Manhattan known as the Lower East Side. If you were to walk down the streets of this neighborhood, you would soon get an idea of how many different peoples live there. Small grocery stores, called *bodegas*, sell plantains and other Latin American specialties. Video stores stock Chinese movies. The sounds of *salsa* and rap music spill onto the sidewalk, where Dominican and Puerto Rican men gather in warm weather to play dominoes.

The Lower East Side has always been the home of immigrants and immigrants' children. This was true in 1930 when Seward Park High School opened. But the mix of peoples then was very different. The Lower East Side of more than sixty years ago was a neighborhood of Italians and Jews. In the apartments that surround the school, foreign-born parents spoke Italian or Yiddish (the language of east European Jews). Shops sold Italian sausages and kosher pickles.

Many population shifts have affected the Lower East Side. In the mid-1800s, before New York City had any public high schools at all, the neighborhood was full of German and Irish immigrants and their children. Amid the neighborhood's tenements stood German beer halls and brand-new churches built by the devoutly Catholic Irish. And in New York's earliest days—before there even was a Lower East Side—its people were mainly Dutch and English.

The Lower East Side is just one neighborhood in one city.

But the changes it has seen are part of a much larger process that has been going on throughout America for hundreds of years. Getting to the United States has been the goal of immigrants since the early 1600s. This was when the English and other Europeans established the first colonies along our country's east coast. Even the Native Americans, who were here long before Europeans came, were immigrants too. The ancestors of today's Native Americans moved into the New World many thousands of years ago, walking across a land bridge from Asia.

Immigrants have come to this country in waves, first from one region of the world and then from another. They became Americans. They built a new nation, the United States, which eventually stretched from the Atlantic to, and into, the Pacific.

Because of its many different peoples, the United States has been called "a nation of nations." One of the country's mottoes is *E pluribus unum*. These Latin words mean "out of many, one." You can read them in the beak of the eagle that appears on a dollar bill.

Our country has also been called a melting pot. Technically a melting pot is a container in which separate materials, usually metals, are heated together. The metals lose their separate identities—such as copper and zinc—and blend into a new substance—such as brass. When people call the United States a melting pot, they are using a metaphor. (A metaphor is a figure of speech in which one thing or idea is used to describe another. Calling a baby a "bundle of joy" is a metaphor.) If we speak of America as a melting pot, we mean that all of its different peoples have been mixed together. They have lost characteristics that made them different and instead blended into something new, something "American."

Take New York City, for example. Did the Germans and the Italians of the Lower East Side, and the Dutch and English before them, lose a part of themselves to blend into something new? Are today's Asians and Hispanics—and Russians and Arabs and Haitians—doing the same thing? In other words, has America indeed been a melting pot? Is it one now? Should it be? These are not idle questions. They have to do with who we are, how we see ourselves as individuals, and what it means to be American.

2

Identity and Belonging

"Do you have any I.D.?" When we're asked that question, we usually fish in a pocket, bag, or backpack and produce a school pass, a library card, or maybe a driver's license or credit card. We know that "I.D." stands for "identity." The paper or card that we carry tells others our name, address, and a few other facts about us. But identity, of course, is more than facts like these.

Nations and Nationality

National identity has to do with the nation, or country, of which we are citizens. The world's present-day population—more than five billion—is divided among about 160 nations. They range from such giants as China and India to tiny places like Singapore and Grenada. When we speak of nationality, we mean citizenship in a given nation. A citizen of France has French nationality, a citizen of Brazil has Brazilian nationality, and so on.

People acquire citizenship in two main ways. One way is by being born in a country. Any child born in the United States is automatically an American citizen. This principle does not apply in many other countries. For instance, a child born in Germany is considered to be of German nationality only if his or her parents are German.

The other way of acquiring citizenship is by naturalization. This is a process whereby an alien, a person born somewhere else, changes nationality. He or she moves to another country as an immigrant—someone intending to stay here. At the same time, the individual is an emigrant from his or her native country—someone leaving it for good.

In the United States, naturalization generally involves (a) living in the country for five years, (b) applying for citizenship, and (c) demonstrating a knowledge of English and of American history in a hearing. The final step is a ceremony in

---

In Their Own Words: National Identity

Sean McGonagle immigrated to the United States in 1966. Here he describes his feelings about his identity as an American:

You know when I first found out that I was getting to be patriotic, if you could call me in any way patriotic? I used to watch these games, like the Olympics, and I found myself jumping with excitement for the Americans to win.[1]

which new citizens take an oath pledging loyalty to the United States. Foreign-born residents of the United States are often spoken of as first-generation Americans. Their children are second-generation Americans and so on.

Race

Although we are born into one nationality, we can change it through naturalization. Race, on the other hand, is something we're born into that we can't change. It consists of physical characteristics that we inherit from our parents.

It is common to divide people into three main racial groups. One group is the Negroid. Most members of this group have dark skin, tightly curled black hair, brown eyes, and full lips. Members of the Mongoloid group usually have yellowish skin, brown eyes, and straight black hair. A special fold in their eyelids makes their eyes look slanted. A third racial group is known as the Caucasoid. Caucasians, or whites, generally have fair skin, straight or curly hair ranging from blond to black, and eyes in a wide range of colors.

A caution: There are millions of people who don't fit exactly into any of these categories. For instance, many Indians of south Asia have dark skin, but Caucasian features. Native Americans and Inuit (Eskimos) belong to the Mongoloid group, as do the Chinese and Japanese. But many Native Americans and Inuit lack the special eyefold of this group.

Race has no scientific meaning at all. Everyone belongs to the same human species, and we are much more alike than different biologically. (People sometimes say that a person has, for instance, "Negro blood," but there is no such thing. The basic blood types occur in all racial groups.) Race, however, does have a *social* meaning. In other words, people *think* it's important, and they attach all sorts of meanings to it. (See "We and They" later in this chapter.)

The United States government classifies people in five "racial" groups: American Indian or Alaskan Native, Asian or Pacific Islander, black, white, and Hispanic. Many scholars criticize these categories as confused and arbitrary. American Indians and Asians belong to the same broad racial stock, while most Hispanics blend different races.[2]

Religion

Our religious identity has to do with what we regard as sacred and how we worship. The so-called "major religions" of the world have ancient traditions and members all over the globe. The major religions include Buddhism, Hinduism, Islam, Judaism, and Christianity, which is divided into Roman Catholicism, Orthodox Catholicism, and numerous Protestant denominations.

There are also hundreds of local religions closely linked to group survival. For instance, among Native Americans, each smaller grouping—the Cherokees, the Sioux, the Navajos, and so on—had (and, in many cases, still has) its own religious traditions. They explained how the group came to be, defined what was holy, and set forth the rituals for worship.

The United States has a long religious tradition. The Pilgrims and Puritans of New England immigrated to America in order to be able to practice their (Protestant) religion freely. Other groups sought similar freedom—so many, in fact, that the colonies became known for their religious toleration. Guaranteed by the Constitution, religious freedom protected the "free exercise" of a wide variety of faiths. However, almost 90 percent of Americans identify themselves as Christians. And, although church and state are officially separate, religion is very much present in American society. The national motto is "In God we trust," each session of Congress opens with a prayer, and Christmas has the status of a national holiday.

In Their Own Words: Racial Identity

Eddy Harris, a young African American, visited twenty-three countries in Africa. This selection from *Native Stranger*, his book about his experiences, expresses some of his feelings about being black:

Black Africa. A quiet sense of elation and something akin to relief swept over me. It wasn't exactly like coming home, but perhaps simply the bracing awareness that upon this same earth a man who looked like me had walked centuries before me. What he saw and what he did was planted in my genes. Something in the soul does not forget. I was in black Africa at last.[3]

Ethnic Groups

Nationality, race, and religion all help shape a person's identity. Together with other characteristics, they also determine the ethnic group to which he or she belongs. An ethnic group consists of people within a larger society who share several traits that tend to unify them and make them feel different from other groups. Members of a given ethnic group come from the same geographic region, have a common history, and usually possess similar physical traits and religious beliefs. In addition, people of the same ethnicity generally speak the same language, share the same values and

---

In Their Own Words:
Religious Identity

Jodi Padnick, an American teenager, lived in Spain as an exchange student. There, for the first time, she became deeply conscious of her Jewishness:

My first Friday in Barcelona, the Sabbath drew near, and I suddenly wanted to be with other Jews. I managed to find a small synagogue where the traditional melodies of the familiar Sabbath prayers reminded me of home. Sitting there, thinking about the great Jewish community of Spain which ended abruptly with their mass expulsion in 1492, I felt a new sense of identification with my people, our faith and shared history.[4]

---

traditions, and maintain similar customs in everyday life—food, music, dances, holidays, and so on. Often they marry people from the same group.

Ethnic groups of Europe include the Lapps of northern Scandinavia and the Basques of Spain. Africa has numerous ethnic groups, including the Masai of the east, the Zulus of the south, and the Ibo of the west.

Because the United States was settled by immigrants from all over the world, it has many ethnic groups. The *Harvard Encyclopedia of American Ethnic Groups* has articles on 106 separate peoples, from Acadians (the French-speaking "Cajuns" of Louisiana) to Zoroastrians (a religious group that began in what is now Iran).[5] Among the largest ethnic groups are African Americans (see Chapter Five) and Hispanic Americans (see Chapter Six). Native Americans form an ethnic group (see Chapter Seven). So do Jews, Chinese, Japanese, Filipinos, Pakistanis, Italians, and Poles—and many others.[6]

All Americans are either immigrants or descended from immigrants. But not all Americans identify themselves with an ethnic group. This is especially true for people with English, Scottish, or Scottish-Irish ancestors. Because these groups were among the first Europeans to settle in our country, and because their traditions were dominant for a long time, they have not felt separate or "different." Indeed, as you will see in Chapters Three and Four, they have tended to think of themselves (and sometimes *only* themselves) as "100 percent Americans." Today they form part of the large group known as WASPs (White Anglo-Saxon Protestants).

One way American ethnic groups celebrate their heritage is by holding parades. For instance, Irish Americans have a parade on St. Patrick's Day, March 17, and Italian Americans have a parade on Columbus Day, October 12. These youngsters are costumed for a celebration of Chinese New Year, which takes place in midwinter.

We and They

What happens when two ethnic groups come into contact with each other? Each may continue to maintain its own culture, or way of life. More often, people of one group take on some of the characteristics of the other—a process known as acculturation. For instance, when people from Spain colonized Latin America, most of its native peoples learned Spanish and adopted Roman Catholicism. In many cases they added these new traits without abandoning their ways.

One ethnic group may adopt so many traits of the other that, practically speaking, it loses its separate identity—a process called assimilation. This happened to various groups from the British Isles when they settled in the English colonies of North America. Within one or two generations, the Welsh and Scottish people, for example, stopped speaking their own dialects and following their own customs. They became part of the general population.

Relations among ethnic groups can be tense and even hostile. All of us differentiate between our own culture and the cultures of others. We tend to think of our own customs as "normal," and regard those of others as "weird," "stupid," or "harmful." The same kinds of we-they feelings affect ethnic relations. We develop stereotypes—oversimplified mental pictures—about people who are different from us. Sometimes a stereotype is positive. More often, a stereotype is negative. A Muslim woman living in the United States comments on a current stereotype she sees among Americans: "They think of a Muslim woman with a huge sheet on and three children trailing behind her, and her trailing behind her husband who just finished beating her."[7]

When we *think* in negative stereotypes, the result is prejudice. If we *act* on our prejudices, the result is discrimination. For example, Joe Smith may think that all Italian Americans are criminals; clearly, he is prejudiced against Italian Americans. If he goes further and refuses to rent an apartment to an Italian family, he is discriminating.

In Their Own Words: Ethnic Identity

George Latsko, a second-generation American, had this to say about his background:

> *I am now twenty years of age and I never get tired of hearing my father tell us different stories and tales of his native Czechoslovakia. He may tell the same story many times . . . but each time makes it more interesting. . . . Much as he would like to, I don't suppose Dad will ever go back to Czechoslovakia. But I have resolved that at the very first opportunity I will go there and see the birthplace of my father, whose word-pictures of the customs, superstitions, and religious views of a hard-working and proud race I shall always retain in my memory.*[8]

Throughout history, majorities have discriminated against minorities. Sometimes religion is the excuse. For centuries, Christians persecuted Jews, holding them responsible for the crucifixion of Christ. Because of anti-Semitism (hostility toward Jews), Jews were expelled from one country after another, forbidden to own land, and kept out of many professions. In many cities, they were forced to live in special districts called ghettos. Discrimination against them reached barbaric levels with the Holocaust during World War II. During this time, Germany's Nazi government deliberately murdered six million Jews.

Race plays a big role in discrimination. Racism, the belief that one race is superior to others, has existed among most peoples of the world. The Chinese, for instance, long regarded themselves as racially better than "round-eyed" Westerners. The Arabs, Europeans, and Americans who enslaved Africans in huge numbers, beginning in the 1500s, justified their cruelty by claiming that whites were racially superior to blacks.

In America white Europeans and their descendants have claimed that they were superior to Native Americans, to blacks, and to Asians. Racism has been particularly strong when different racial groups were seen as competing for the same land, jobs, or status. At various times in our history—as you will read in Chapters Five, Six, and Seven—racism has justified terrible acts of discrimination.

chapter 3

Streams of Settlers

Today approximately two hundred fifty million people live in the United States.[1] Our country, the fourth largest in the world, is a modern industrial nation, in which big cities and their sprawling suburbs are linked by highways and complex communication networks. It's hard to imagine what America was like before it was "discovered" by Europeans some five hundred years ago.

Of course, America had been "discovered" centuries earlier by the ancestors of today's Native Americans. But they were not numerous in the area that would later become the United States. They lived in small communities scattered among the region's vast forests, plains, and mountains.

Europeans, coming from a crowded continent, looked upon America as an empty land. To them, this spacious New World spelled opportunity. John Smith, an English explorer of the east coast, wrote: "Who can but approve this a most excellent place, both for health and fertility? Of all the four parts of the world I have yet seen not inhabited, could I have but means to transport a colony, I would rather live here than anywhere."[2]

Early Colonists

The first people of European descent to live in our country came from Spain or its possessions in the Caribbean and Mexico. Some of them settled in what is now Florida and some of them settled in the Southwest. Other Europeans, from France or its possessions in Canada, settled along the Great Lakes and the Mississippi River. None of these regions, however, was part of the United States as it was first founded. Our country grew out of English colonies established along the Atlantic coast.

The first permanent English settlements were established in Virginia (1607) and Massachusetts (1620). Over the next several decades, other colonies took shape until there were thirteen, from New Hampshire in the North to Georgia in the South. Colonial population grew steadily, totaling about two hundred fifty thousand by 1700 and over one million by 1750.[3] Although people had big families in those days, much of the increase was due to immigration.

After the United States won its independence from Great Britain, it took its first official census. This population count revealed that the new republic had almost four million inhabitants. Of these, almost half were English or of English descent. The next biggest group were blacks from Africa, most of them slaves. Other peoples included Scotch-Irish, Germans, Scottish, French, Irish, and Dutch.[4]

English influence was very strong in shaping the new nation. The English language was spoken almost everywhere. The English system of law was also in widespread use. As in England, the dominant religious tradition was Protestant. English ideals of liberty, toleration, and self-government were the foundations of the Declaration of Independence and the Constitution.

New Arrivals

Immigration laws adopted by the young United States were the most liberal in the world. They placed few restrictions on immigrants, and made naturalization easy. Because of this, newcomers came in growing numbers. The census, which first started to keep track of immigration in 1820, recorded a tenfold increase between that date and 1840.[5]

The 1840s saw an even bigger jump in immigration. One important factor was a disease that killed much of the potato crop in Ireland—a crop on which Irish peasants relied for their basic food. Thousands starved to death and thousands fled to the United States. More than six hundred fifty thousand "famine Irish" came to America in the 1840s, one million in the 1850s.[6]

Another major source of immigration in the mid-1800s was Germany. When revolutions there failed, people involved in the uprisings were afraid of being imprisoned or executed.

Most Irish immigrants who came to the United States in the wake of the potato famine settled in slums where dirt and disease were common. The artist who drew this sketch called it a "Court for King Cholera" — in other words, a likely location for the deadly disease.

Many escaped. Almost one million Germans migrated to America in the 1850s.[7]

A third region that sent many immigrants was Scandinavia. Norway, Sweden, and their neighbors were very poor in the 1800s, and many farm families had no land of their own. Cheap fares advertised by American steamship and rail lines attracted thousands to the fertile acres of the Midwest.

The newcomers of this period changed the population mix in the United States. The so-called "native" Americans—immigrants who had come here starting in the 1600s—were especially distressed by the Irish, and to a lesser extent, the Germans and Scandinavians. The Irish were poor, often illiterate, and Catholic. (Anti-Catholicism had been widespread in America since the days of the first English colonists.) The Germans and Scandinavians, though mostly middle class and Protestant, did not speak English. Because members of each group liked to settle together, they were accused of clannishness.

Anti-immigrant feeling, or nativism, led to discrimination, especially against the Irish. Typical was this 1853 advertisement: "Woman Wanted. To do general housework . . . English, Scotch, Welsh, German, or any country or color except Irish."[8] Nativists formed several organizations whose aims were to restrict immigration and make naturalization harder. Their organized efforts resulted in no laws at this time, but nativism remained a strong force in American society.

Beginning in the late 1800s, immigrants started coming in huge numbers from areas of Europe that had not contributed many immigrants before—Russia, Poland, Austria-Hungary, Italy, and Greece. These Europeans are often known as "new immigrants," in contrast to the "old immigrants" from Ireland, Germany, and Scandinavia. The period from 1900 to 1914 saw the heaviest influx of newcomers in American history—over one million a year in several years.[9]

The "new immigrants" aroused a great deal of nativist feeling. They spoke foreign languages and tended to be poor and unskilled. Many of them were Catholic. There were also thousands of Jews, whose Yiddish language and Jewish religion struck so-called "native" Americans as strange and even threatening.

Equally strange and threatening to Americans on the west coast were the increasing numbers of Chinese immigrants. Most were men, recruited to work on the transcontinental railroads beginning in the 1860s. After the railroads were built, these immigrants settled in urban Chinese communities (Chinatowns), where they kept their languages and customs.

What Then Is the American?

Its many streams of settlers made the United States different from most other countries. Even before the nation became independent, its people had begun to see themselves as special, as *Americans.* They came from so many different places that they could not be identified with any single ethnic group. A French immigrant, Hector St. John de Crèvecoeur, wrote in the 1770s:

What then is the American, this new man? He is either an European, or the descendant of an European, hence that strange mixture of blood, which you will find in no other country. I could point out to you a family whose grandfather was an Englishman, whose wife was Dutch, whose son married a French woman, and whose present four sons have now four wives of different nations.[10]

Later observers noted the same variety. The writer Ralph Waldo Emerson spoke of America as an "asylum of [safe place for] all nations, the energy of Irish, Germans, Swedes, Poles, & Cossacks, & all the European tribes—of the Africans, & of the Polynesians."[11]

In America all these different individuals were "melted into a new race of men," as Crèvecoeur put it. (Emerson spoke of a "smelting pot.") How did this process work? The basic idea was that newcomers were expected to abandon their old ways. In George Washington's words, immigrants were to abandon the "language, habits and principles (good or bad) which they bring with them." Then they could be "assimilated to our customs, measures, and laws: in a word, soon become *one people.*"[12] John Adams advised that foreigners "must cast off the European skin, never to resume it."[13]

In place of their old ways, immigrants were expected to adopt the customs of their new home. They were to learn English, to obey the laws, and to respect American traditions of toleration and freedom, whether or not they actually became citizens and voted. As one writer put it, "The ideals, the

27

opportunities . . . of our democracy change the immigrants into a new order of men."[14]

For many decades people assumed that acculturation would happen naturally and spontaneously, aided to a large extent by free public education. And this seemed to happen, mainly because the immigrants themselves wanted to be "American." One Irish immigrant wrote home:

> *The second generation here are not interested in their ancestors. We have never told them of the realities of life . . . over there, and would not encourage any of them to visit. . . . When we left there, we left the old world behind, we are all American citizens and proud of it.*[15]

Newcomers might cling to their old ways for a time. A German immigrant wrote in 1848:

> *We build for ourselves American homes, but within glows a German hearth. We wear American hats, but under them are German eyes looking out from a German face . . . We live according to American habits but we hold fast to German morals.*[16]

With time, however, old traditions died out. In the case of Germany (which sent more immigrants to the United States than any other single country), acculturation worked in a special way. Americans adopted so many German customs that the customs stopped being German. This is true of everything from hot dogs and kindergartens to Christmas trees and New Year's eve celebrations—not to mention *"Gesundheit!"* (German for "good health") when we sneeze.

The same process of acculturation took place among "new

immigrants." In New York City, where thousands of Jewish immigrants had settled, an observer noted in 1905:

> *English is more and more the language spoken on the East Side, whereas eight years ago it was rare to hear that tongue; today American clothes are worn, whereas in years gone by, persons used to go to the East Side out of curiosity to see the foreign dress.*[17]

Immigrants, or their children or grandchildren, not only learned English; they usually stopped speaking their native language. They moved out of the neighborhoods where they had clustered together. Many changed their names, a process that had been going on for centuries. Earlier the Roggenfelders had become Rockefellers and the Rivoires had become Reveres. In the 1900s the process continued. Israel Baline wrote songs as Irving Berlin, Michael Peschkowsky directed plays as Mike Nichols, and Frank Perdeaux sold millions of chickens as Frank Perdue.

The Melting Pot

On an October evening in 1908, a new play opened in Washington, D.C. Wild applause at the end brought the playwright, an Englishman of Jewish descent named Israel Zangwill, on stage. As he appeared, President Theodore Roosevelt called out from his box, "That's a great play, Mr. Zangwill!"

Zangwill's drama, *The Melting-Pot*, was about a Russian-Jewish composer in New York, David Quixano, and his love for a young Christian from Russia, Vera Revendal. Because of

29

David's belief in America's power to blend conflicting elements, the two young people are able to triumph over family opposition. The final scene takes place on the rooftop of a building in lower Manhattan. Gesturing toward the city, David says:

> There she lies, the great Melting-Pot—listen! Can't you hear the roaring and the bubbling? . . . Ah, what a stirring and a seething! Celt and Latin, Slav and Teuton, Greek and Syrian—black and yellow—
>
> VERA: (Softly, nestling to him): Jew and Gentile—
>
> DAVID: Yes, East and West, and North and South, the palm and the pine, the pole and the equator, the crescent and the cross. . . . Here shall they all unite to build the Republic of Man and the Kingdom of God. Ah, Vera, what is the glory of Rome and Jerusalem where all nations and races come to worship and look back, compared with the glory of America, where all races and nations come to labour and look forward!. . .
>
> *(Far back, like a lonely, guiding star, twinkles over the darkening water the torch of the Statue of Liberty. From below comes up the softened sound of voices and instruments joining in "My Country, 'tis of Thee." The curtain falls slowly.)*[18]

Roosevelt and many other Americans liked Zangwill's play because it dramatized the way they wanted to think of America and its mission. Zangwill popularized an idea that had long been common but not so clearly expressed. If the United States was indeed a melting pot, it would absorb and painlessly transform all immigrants into Americans. In the process, the newcomers would be perfected, as smelting removes impurities from metals. The reality was more complicated. For many, becoming American was very hard. And for some, particularly those of different races, it was just about impossible.

Restrictions on Immigration

Even as Americans welcomed the melting-pot idea, they were working to change their liberal immigration policies. Anti-foreign feeling was strong in the late 1800s and early 1900s. It was fed not only by a surge in immigration but by other factors too. Many Americans worried that foreigners would take their jobs. Strikes and other labor unrest were blamed on foreigners. The assassination of President William McKinley by a Polish-American radical added to antiforeign feeling. So did so-called "scientific" theories about the superiority of the Anglo-Saxon "race."[19] (This was also a time of increased discrimination against African Americans, as you will read in Chapter Five.)

The first antiforeign restrictions were directed against immigrants from Asia. In 1882 Congress passed the Chinese Exclusion Act, the first American law aimed against one specific nationality. It prohibited all Chinese immigration for ten years, and was later renewed. Early in the 1900s Congress also limited the number of Japanese immigrants.

Restrictions against European immigrants began with laws against admitting people suffering from "a loathsome or dangerous contagious disease."[20] In 1917 Congress adopted other restrictions. Immigrants had to pay a fee, provide a birth certificate, and prove that they could read and write.

In 1921 the government adopted the first quota law, which limited the number of European newcomers allowed into the country. Another law in 1924 halved this total. This law also set limits that drastically reduced immigration from eastern and southern Europe. In 1921, for instance, Italian immigration totaled over two hundred twenty thousand. The following year the number was about forty thousand.[21] The door that had stood open for decades was beginning to swing shut.

Changing Times

"When I young fellow I felt that I American," said a Chinese-born California merchant in 1924. "Now I got more sense. I know I never be American, always Chinaman. I no care now anymore."[1]

Pany Lowe spoke for many immigrants of his time. The melting pot didn't work for everyone. And even when it seemed to, the cost could be very high.

Tears and Troubles in the "Golden Land"

Before they left home, immigrants heard all sorts of rumors about the wealth they would find in America. It was said that coins lay about everywhere, that the streets themselves were paved with gold. Jews called America the "golden land"; the Chinese knew it as the "golden mountain."

Of course the reality was different. Many immigrants— such as the Irish and central and southern Europeans—were unskilled peasants. They had to take whatever jobs they could find, building railroads and subways, shoveling coal in factories, or plowing and harvesting on farms. They worked long hours at low pay. A young Irish woman wrote home to friends: "it is not so very easey to get Muney heer as we all [thought] when [we] were to home; you have to work hard to make one pound."[2]

Living conditions were primitive, especially in crowded city slums. Jane Addams, who founded the famous Chicago settlement house known as Hull House, wrote of Chicago in the early 1900s:

> *The streets are inexpressibly dirty, the number of schools inadequate, sanitary legislation unenforced, the street lighting bad, the paving miserable and altogether lacking in the alleys and smaller streets, and the stables foul beyond description. Hundreds of houses are unconnected with the street sewer.*[3]

While conditions like these faced Americans born in this country as well, immigrants coped with special problems. Uprooted from their communities, most had to learn a new language and new customs. Many were so unhappy and homesick that they gave up; according to one estimate, a third of all immigrants returned to their native lands.[4]

For newcomers who remained, prejudice and discrimination were common. Ugly nicknames were coined for every ethnic group: Jews were "sheenies" and "kikes"; Italians were "wops" and "dagoes"; other Europeans were singled out as "polacks" (Polish), "bohunks" (Bohemians), and "squareheads"

(Swedes). A foreign accent or name might keep an immigrant from being hired, finding a place to live, or obtaining credit.

Insults and discrimination were bad enough. But even worse was the damage to immigrants' very identity. In the late 1800s, when antiforeign feeling was running high, many Americans decided that the melting pot wasn't working fast enough on its own. It needed help. Their answer was "Americanization"—a conscious effort to speed up assimilation.

Americanization involved English classes, patriotic pageants, and awards for "good citizenship." It also encouraged conscious rejection of a foreigner's past. A group of newly naturalized citizens was lectured by President Woodrow Wilson in 1915: "You cannot become thorough Americans if you think of yourselves in groups.... A man who thinks of himself as belonging to a particular national group in America has not yet become an American."[5] According to one Jewish newcomer:

> *We were "Americanized" about as gently as horses are broken in. In the whole crude process, we sensed a disrespect for the alien traditions in our homes and came unconsciously to resent and despise those traditions, good and bad alike, because they seemed insuperable barriers between ourselves and our adopted land.*[6]

This story was even sadder from a parent's point of view, especially since so many had sacrificed everything for their children. The old man who wrote the following passage was born in Lithuania:

My children have grown up. They are educated, and the education given them by America has taken them from me. I speak English only as an untaught alien can speak it. But my children know all the slang phrases. They speak differently, they act differently, and when they come to visit me they come alone. They do not explain why they do not bring their friends, but I instinctively sense the reason. They should not fear. I would not cause them any embarrassment. But they too look upon their old father as an inferior, an alien.[7]

Mixed Signals

The period around the time of World War II was one of mixed signals where ethnicity was concerned. (Interestingly, the first recorded use of the word in its current usage dates from 1941.) In the 1930s, textbooks and other educational materials began to call attention to the positive accomplishments of various immigrants. They noted, for example, that the Irish had almost singlehandedly created a Roman Catholic church organization in America. And they praised the contributions of outstanding individuals like inventor Alexander Graham Bell (from Scotland), physicist Albert Einstein (from Germany), football coach Knute Rockne (from Norway), and conductor Arturo Toscanini (from Italy).

Symbolic of this trend was a change in attitudes toward the Statue of Liberty. When it was dedicated in 1886, and for years afterward, the statue symbolized the friendship between France and the United States. Only in the 1930s did the statue come to stand for America's welcome to strangers. And

CHINESE • GERMAN • CZECHO-SLOVAKIAN • BRAZIL • SPANISH • JEWISH • SCOTCH • ROUMANIAN • ENGLISH •

• AUSTRIAN • SLAVIC • ITALIAN • POLISH • RUSSIAN • TURK • GREEK • IRISH • LITHUNIAN • PORTUGES

In the 1920s, when these photographs were taken, immigrants were encouraged to think of themselves as blending into a melting pot. Note that while most of the girls identify themselves by nationality, some prefer religion (Jewish), or language (Slavic).

not until 1945 was the famous poem by Emma Lazarus moved from an upper landing of the statue to the main entrance. (Lazarus' reference to immigrants as "wretched refuse" indicates Americans' feelings about the "new immigration" of the late 1800s, when the poem was written.)[8]

Antiforeign prejudice was diminishing. Because of the Nazis' persecution of the Jews, American anti-Semitism declined. (The United States, however, took in very few Jewish refugees from Europe.) During the Great Depression and World War II, Americans developed feelings of solidarity as they fought common enemies. American war movies featuring combat troops typically depicted a "melting-pot" group of buddies. Among the favorites were Jews or Italians from Brooklyn, Scandinavian farmers from the Plains, Polish Americans from Chicago, and New Englanders of English descent.

The war years, however, also witnessed one of the worst antiforeign episodes in American history. This was the period of the internment (imprisonment) of 110,000 Japanese Americans—two-thirds of them citizens—in relocation camps. The authorities' excuse was that Japanese Americans lived near the west coast, where they might aid potential Japanese invaders. But racism certainly played a part in this decision. No actions were taken against Americans of German or Italian descent, in spite of the fact that Germany and Italy were also enemy nations.

When ordered to the camps, Japanese Americans had to sell their land and houses at rock-bottom prices. No one was ever even accused of disloyal actions. In fact, many

Japanese-American men joined the United States Army. Finally, in the 1980s, Congress admitted that a "grave injustice" had been committed. The United States government awarded $20,000 tax-free to each living former internee.

The federal government passed a new immigration law in 1952. It removed an earlier ban on Asian immigrants. But it kept in place the system of quotas that had been established in the 1920s.

The Ethnic Revival

In 1960, for the first time in its history, the United States chose a Roman Catholic as President. The election of John Fitzgerald Kennedy, the grandson of Irish immigrants, indicated the weakening of anti-Catholic prejudice. Even bigger changes were to follow.

One important change was a new immigration law, passed in 1965. It did away with the old system of quotas that favored immigrants from Europe. Instead, the law emphasized uniting families. It allowed more newcomers from the western hemisphere and from Asia, and also increased the yearly total. Other changes involved African Americans. A civil rights movement, led by Martin Luther King, Jr., had begun in the late 1950s. It reached a high point in the mid-1960s, with the passage of laws outlawing many forms of racial discrimination. Soon afterward a more militant "Black Power" crusade served to strengthen blacks' ethnic identity. An outgrowth of these developments was affirmative action—active recruitment of African Americans in jobs and education. (You will read more about these developments in Chapter Five.)

Affirmative action applied not just to African Americans but also to other groups that had suffered discrimination, such as women and minorities. (A minority is a group of people singled out for less than equal treatment in a society.) Two important minorities—Hispanics and Native Americans—were among those who also qualified for affirmative action (see Chapters Six and Seven).

The emphasis on ethnicity also affected the so-called "white ethnics"—Americans of southern and eastern European descent. Many formed organizations to represent their interests. One, for instance, was the American Italian Historical Association. Another was the Czechoslovak History Conference. Schools and colleges revised curriculums to call attention to America's multiethnic reality. Mass-media entertainment and advertising reflected this diversity.

In 1972 the government adopted the Ethnic Heritage Studies Program. It allotted federal funds for curriculum materials and teacher training so that students could learn more about the contributions of their own and other ethnic groups. As the ethnic revival progressed, ethnicity came to be seen as a core American value, along with democracy and freedom.

Two main forces lay behind the ethnic revival. One was a reaction against Americanization, or, as it is sometimes called, Anglo-conformity. As the latter term indicates, Americanization was viewed as forced assimilation to a culture based on English (that is, WASP) traditions. Leaders of the ethnic revival wanted to broaden the meaning of "American." The term should not be reserved only for those descended from English or northern European ancestors. It should also be applied to people of African, Asian, Native-American, and Latin-American descent.

The second force behind the ethnic revival was a loss of confidence in the American system as a whole. Millions of Americans disagreed with government policy in Vietnam, where the United States fought a long, costly, and losing war. Another concern was the Watergate scandal, which forced President Richard Nixon out of office in 1974. Events like these weakened Americans' sense of patriotism and their trust in traditional values. These were linked to "Anglo-conformity." People from other ethnic backgrounds could stress their different ethnicities. This made them feel less responsible for a system of which they disapproved.[9]

Orchestra, Salad, or What?

The ethnic revival, with its emphasis on the positive side of cultural differences, had some roots in the past. Way back in 1915, an American philosopher named Horace Kallen had published a magazine article titled "Democracy Versus the Melting Pot." To be truly democratic, he said, the United States should stop trying to force everyone into an "Anglo-Saxon" mold. Instead it should encourage each ethnic group to emphasize its own heritage.

Kallen called his alternative "cultural pluralism." It was not popular when he first wrote about it, but it became popular in the 1960s. Today people mean essentially the same thing when they speak of cultural diversity or multiculturalism.

Whatever term people used, one fact was certain: the melting-pot metaphor had lost its appeal. An influential book of 1963, written by Nathan Glazer and Daniel Moynihan, was called *Beyond the Melting Pot.* Its authors, investigating ethnicity in New York City, found that African Americans, Jews, Italians, and others each maintained a group identity. "The point about the melting pot," Glazer and Moynihan wrote in their preface, "is that it did not happen."[10]

Other books from this period carried a similar message. *The Rise of the Unmeltable Ethnics* focused on non-English Europeans. The title of *The Decline of the WASP* said it all.[11] An Italian American at a 1971 conference called the melting-pot idea "a myth which has been perpetuated by the elite-dominated American educational system to commit cultural genocide on our people."[12] The Polish-American congressman who sponsored the Ethnic Heritage Studies bill stated, "I find the whole doctrine of the melting pot frankly very repugnant. I don't want to be melted down."[13]

If the United States isn't a melting pot, what is it? People have suggested several other metaphors. Kallen liked the idea of an orchestra. "As every type [of instrument] has its appropriate theme and melody in the whole symphony, so in society, each ethnic group may be the natural instrument, its temper and culture may be its theme and melody and the harmony and dissonances and discords of them all may make the symphony of civilization."[14] Other metaphors include a mosaic, a salad bowl, and a rainbow.

Historian Lawrence Fuchs, the grandson of immigrants, finds fault with all of these. A symphony implies near perfect harmony, he says, and a mosaic is too static. In a salad bowl, the ingredients do not change, while a rainbow disappears. He prefers to think of a kaleidoscope, where the parts constantly shift to form new patterns.[15] We'll come back to the question of the melting pot in Chapter Eight, after looking at the ethnic experience of three groups in our society.

chapter

5

African Americans and The Ethnic Experience

"I am the darker brother," wrote the African-American poet Langston Hughes; "I, too, am American."[1] It took centuries for the people of the United States to recognize this brotherhood—to see their "darker brothers" as Americans.

African Americans form the largest minority in the United States today. They number about thirty million—around 12 percent of the total population.[2] Many more Americans probably have African-American ancestors.

The Uprooted

Almost all African Americans are descended from Africans who were brought to America as slaves. In Africa, as elsewhere in the world, slavery had its roots deep in the past. Many different African groups had slaves. The people enslaved were either war prisoners, criminals, or debtors. They were attached to and lived alongside the large families that were common in Africa. And they had certain rights. For instance, they could usually marry, own property, and buy their freedom. Generally their children were not considered slaves.

In the 1500s Europeans began exploiting the riches of the New World. Facing a labor shortage, they first enslaved Native Americans. But the Native Americans died in great numbers, mainly because they were not immune to the new diseases introduced by Europeans. So Europeans turned to Africans, who had been exposed to these diseases over the centuries. Slavery in America was a harsh system, with gangs of workers employed in fields and mines under strict overseers. In general slaves had few, if any, rights, and their children were born into the same condition.

Most American slaves came from West Africa. Coastal groups helped capture other peoples from the interior in order to sell them to foreign slave traders. No one knows how many Africans were sent to America. One expert gives the total as about ten million; of this number, about four hundred thousand came to the British colonies of mainland North America.[3] Thousands died in captivity in Africa, thousands more on the atrociously overcrowded slave ships.

Surviving Slavery

The United States was founded on the principle of individual liberty. The Declaration of Independence proclaimed that "all men are created equal." How then could slavery be right? In general Americans justified slavery by claiming that black people were inferior to whites, unable to handle the responsibilities of citizenship. In 1808 the United States did outlaw the slave trade, but not slavery. By this time, African Americans totaled more than one million—about a fifth of the population.[4] The vast majority of them lived as slaves in the South, where they worked mainly as farmhands tending fields of rice, tobacco, sugar cane, and cotton.

Slaves were an economic investment for their owners and were needed for their labor. But slaves' work was hard, and they were given only inferior cabins, coarse clothing, and monotonous food. Family members were often separated from each other. Few slaves learned to read and write. (Teaching them was illegal in many places.) They faced severe punishment, even death, if they rebelled or tried to escape.

Africans in America underwent many changes. They had to adjust to a harsh way of life that allowed them no rights whatsoever and no chance to improve their situation. They learned a new language, English. Slaves came from many different tribal groups with many different languages, so they had to adopt a common tongue in order to speak with each other. Slaves also converted to Protestant Christianity. Slave owners encouraged conversion because they thought it would make slaves more obedient. In any case, it would have been difficult for Africans to preserve their native religions because they were linked with specific tribal groups in specific African locations. Slaves also became racially mixed. White slave owners had children with black slaves. And some slaves escaped to Native-American settlements, and they intermarried with Native Americans.

Although African Americans had to abandon much of

Southern slave owners, like the one shown here at center, encouraged Christian worship among their slaves. At a time when few slaves could receive an education, preachers were among the few African Americans who could read and write.

their culture, they kept some traits, often mixing them with elements of New World customs. For instance, their way of speaking English (known today as black English) combined English words with the grammar of various African languages.[5] African Americans also introduced several African words into English, including banana, banjo, gumbo, okra, and tote. In African-American churches, the call-and-response form of preaching and singing was typical of Africa. Slaves developed a kind of hymn, the Negro spiritual, that used biblical imagery to express their longing for freedom.

Not all African Americans were slaves. In 1820 there were over two-hundred thousand free blacks in the United States—about 13 percent of the total African-American population.[6] Some had been freed when the northern states abolished slavery in the late 1700s. Others had been freed by their southern owners (often in their wills). Free blacks were discriminated against almost everywhere. Restrictions limited where they could live and the work they could do. Most states prohibited them from voting. Racism was partly to blame. So was fear of economic competition.

Toward Freedom

As time passed, a growing number of Americans began to protest against the evils of slavery. Some people thought that the best solution would be to establish colonies for freed slaves in Africa. Slaveowners, it was believed, would free their slaves more readily if the freed slaves had a place to go—outside the United States. A leader in the African colonization movement was Paul Cuffe, a free black merchant from Massachusetts. At his own expense, he moved thirty-eight free blacks to Sierra Leone, where Britain was settling blacks discharged from its armed forces. Cuffe's action helped inspire the formation of the American Colonization Society in 1817. This group settled several thousand African Americans in what became the African country of Liberia.

African colonization had much more support from whites than it did from blacks. Most blacks simply did not want to move to Africa, a continent they had never seen. "We will never separate ourselves voluntarily from the slave population in this country," declared a convention of free blacks in 1817. "They are our brethren."[7]

A much stronger movement, among both blacks and whites, was abolition — freedom for the slaves. An abolition campaign began in the late 1700s. But it did not gain much support until the 1830s. A major figure was a white journalist named William Lloyd Garrison. In fiery language, his newspaper, the *Liberator*, attacked slavery as an evil that did untold harm not just to blacks but to whites and to American society in general. Other prominent white abolitionists included the poet John Greenleaf Whittier, Theodore Dwight Weld, and Harriet Beecher Stowe. (Stowe's novel, *Uncle Tom's Cabin*, did much to publicize the abolitionists' cause.)

One outstanding black abolitionist was Frederick Douglass, an escaped slave and spellbinding speaker. Another speaker who captivated audiences was an ex-slave named

Isabella. She was a deeply religious woman who renamed herself Sojourner Truth.

Abolitionists not only wrote and lectured against slavery. They also ran the so-called "underground railroad." This network of safe houses enabled slaves to escape from the South to Canada, where slavery was illegal. A leading "conductor" was Harriet Tubman, who is said to have guided more than three hundred slaves to safety.

The abolition movement aroused strong opposition in the South, where publications like the *Liberator* were banned. Many northerners opposed abolition too. They thought emancipation (freedom) should come gradually. Racial bias also made them fearful of blacks living in their midst; even some white abolitionists felt this way.

The slavery issue was a major cause of the Civil War, which began in 1861. At first the aim of the North was not to end slavery but to restore the Union, from which the Confederate states had seceded (withdrawn). But after President Abraham Lincoln issued the Emancipation Proclamation in 1863, it was clear that slavery would end when the North won. African Americans helped achieve this victory. Over 185,000 served in the Union Army. African-American troops saw action in every campaign of the war, and over 38,000 lost their lives.[8]

Years of Hardship

After the war ended in 1865, two new amendments to the Constitution made all African Americans citizens and granted

African-American men the right to vote. (No American women of any race could vote at this time.) Unfortunately the government offered little economic help to the 3,500,000 former slaves who found themselves with no land and few skills. Most of them remained in the South, where they worked as sharecroppers. This meant that they farmed land belonging to others (sometimes their former masters). Instead of paying rent, they turned over a share of the harvested crop.

For a few years after the war, blacks were able to vote and even hold political office. But whites were not about to give up the power they had always wielded over blacks. Organizations such as the Ku Klux Klan used violence to keep the former slaves "in their place."

Beginning in the late 1800s, southern states passed so-called "Jim Crow" laws aimed at complete segregation (separation) of blacks from whites. Blacks had to attend separate schools, ride in separate railroad cars, eat in separate restaurants, and even drink from separate water fountains. The United States Supreme Court ruled that separate facilities for blacks were legal if they were equal to those for whites, but they rarely were. Through trickery and fraud, blacks lost the right to vote throughout the South. Blacks accused of crimes were often denied a fair trial and brutally lynched—hanged or burned alive by mobs.

In this grim time one prominent African American, Booker T. Washington, advised patience and hard work. "No race can prosper till it learns that there is as much dignity in tilling a field as in writing a poem," he said in an 1895 speech.

"It is at the bottom of life we must begin, and not at the top. Nor should we permit our grievances to overshadow our opportunities."[9]

Other African Americans, however, urged a more aggressive approach. Their leader, W.E.B. Du Bois, urged them to demand full political and social equality. Du Bois was one of the founders of the first effective organization to fight for African-American rights, the National Association for the Advancement of Colored People (NAACP).

World War I and its aftermath led to a big change for African Americans. During the war and the prosperous years afterward, northern factories needed workers. Thousands of African Americans moved northward to get better jobs and live in a less racist society. In 1910, 90 percent of African Americans lived in the South. By 1960, well over half lived in the North.[10]

The so-called Great Migration did not put an end to lynchings, race riots, or discrimination. In the northern cities where most migrants settled, they were forced into ghetto slums. But the Great Migration did help produce a community of African-American writers, artists, and musicians. Because so many of them lived in Harlem, the movement is usually known as the Harlem Renaissance. Major figures included the poets Claude McKay and Countee Cullen and the novelist-essayist-poet Langston Hughes.

The 1920s were a time when, as Hughes put it, "the Negro was in vogue." Concert singers like Marian Anderson and Paul Robeson captivated audiences with their programs of Negro spirituals. Even more popular were the legendary musicians who performed such typically African-American music as the blues (Bessie Smith), gospel (Marion Williams), and jazz (Louis Armstrong and Duke Ellington).

A unique voice of the 1920s was that of Marcus Garvey. He was a Jamaican-born leader who founded the United Negro Improvement Association. Garvey praised everything black, insisting that blackness stood for strength and beauty. "The NAACP wants us all to become white by amalgamation [complete assimilation]," he wrote, "but they are not honest enough to come out with the truth. To be a Negro is no disgrace, but an honor."[11] Garvey's solution—a black empire in Africa, with himself as ruler—did not appeal to most African Americans. But they did like his stress on racial pride and they joined his organization by the thousands. Garvey, however, was eventually convicted of mail fraud, imprisoned, and deported back to Jamaica.

Struggle, Achievement, Challenge

Beginning in the 1940s, African Americans made substantial progress in achieving first-class citizenship. An order issued during World War II helped lessen the racial discrimination that had kept African Americans out of high-paying defense jobs. African-American men and women who went to war—about a million—had to serve in segregated units. (Even Red Cross blood banks separated "black" from "white" blood.) Three years after the war, however, the armed forces were finally desegregated.

One target of civil rights protesters was the southern lunch counter, often out of bounds for blacks. Blacks (and whites) who demonstrated by requesting service were often met with violence, or, as shown here, were doused with sugar, ketchup, and mustard.

A big breakthrough of the 1950s was a decision by the Supreme Court of the United States in *Brown* v. *Board of Education.* In this 1954 ruling, the Court decreed that segregated schools were unconstitutional. This decision overturned the earlier "separate but equal" doctrine. It encouraged many Americans, white as well as black, to work for widespread integration—full equality for blacks within mainstream American society. The most prominent spokesman for integration was a Baptist clergyman, Martin Luther King, Jr. He believed that the best way to end segregation was to challenge the United States to live up to its democratic ideals. And the best way to challenge authority, he thought, was through peaceful demonstrations. The crusade led by King was known as the civil rights movement. It mobilized blacks and whites to protest segregated facilities and the denial of voting rights. In a famous speech in Washington, D.C., in 1963, Martin Luther King declared:

> *We can never be satisfied as long as our children are stripped of their selfhood and robbed of their dignity by signs saying "for whites only." We cannot be satisfied as long as the Negro in Mississippi cannot vote and the Negro in New York believes he has nothing for which to vote.*[12]

Among the most important achievements of the civil rights movement were two new laws. The Civil Rights Act of 1964 forbade discrimination in most public accommodations. And the Voting Rights Act of 1965 made it possible for thousands of African Americans in the South to vote for the first time.

A major result of the civil rights movement was an increase in African-American political participation. The 1965 law added two million new African-American voters. In 1968 only 250 African Americans held elective office in the South. Ten years later the total had increased to 2,000.[13] Notable leaders included Thurgood Marshall, the first African-American Justice on the Supreme Court; Carl Stokes, the first African-American mayor of a major city (Cleveland); and Andrew Young, the first African American to serve as ambassador to the United Nations.

In spite of their political progress, African Americans still had far to go. A lot of them lacked jobs and decent incomes. Many had to settle in crime-ridden ghettos, where housing and schools were poor. Such frustrations had helped shape another African-American leader of the 1950s, a man whose message was very different from that of King. Born Malcolm Little, he converted to the Nation of Islam (Black Muslims) while in prison. At that time he changed his name to Malcolm X. Nonviolence was not for Malcolm X. "If someone puts his hand on you," he said, "send him to the cemetery." Nor was integration his goal. "I believe the best solution is complete separation, with our people going back home, to our own African homeland."[14] Malcolm spoke of whites as "devils," although he modified his view after a pilgrimage to Islam's holiest shrine, Mecca. There he was impressed by light- and dark-skinned Muslims worshipping together.

Both Malcolm X and King were assassinated in the 1960s. There were positive trends during this time, however. One, affirmative action, increased African-American enrollment in higher education and training for careers. It also stimulated the hiring of more African Americans in business and industry. Another trend was a new spirit of ethnic pride. "Black is beautiful," proclaimed a popular slogan. Signs of change were everywhere. There was a new awareness of a common past, even though it had been a time of suffering. African-American studies programs in schools and colleges stressed African contributions to world culture. The term "Negro" was discarded in favor of "black." (In the 1980s many Americans of color came to prefer "African American.")[15]

Many African Americans, who wanted to rid themselves of the "slave names" given them by white masters, renamed themselves. This was especially common among Black Muslims. For instance, Cassius Clay became Muhammad Ali and Lew Alcindor became Kareem Abdul Jabbar. Instead of straightening their hair to make it look like white people's hair, many blacks left it tightly curled in a "natural" (or "Afro") or wore African-style braids. African clothing, especially *dashikis* and *kente* cloth, became stylish. "Soul food"—southern specialties such as greens, ham hocks, and black-eyed peas—found favor among whites as well as blacks. American blacks even created a new holiday, Kwanzaa, a harvest festival with African roots.

By the late 1900s, African Americans had clearly established their identity as an ethnic group. But their feelings about American society, and their place in it, were mixed. One path, the path of separatism, was taken by W.E.B. Du Bois. After decades of struggle he became a Communist, renounced his American citizenship, and moved to Ghana. He died there in 1963, one day before the historic civil rights march on Washington. "I was not an American," he said before leaving the United States, but "a colored man in a white world."[16]

A very different attitude was that of L. Douglas Wilder, who in 1989 became the first African American to be elected governor of a state (Virginia).

> *As a boy, when I would read about an Abraham Lincoln or a Thomas Jefferson or about a George Mason, when I would read that all men are created equal and that they are endowed by their creator with certain inalienable rights . . . I knew it meant me.*[17]

6

Hispanic Americans and The Ethnic Experience

One December day in 1993, a well-dressed woman named Alina Fernandez Revuelta stepped off a plane in Atlanta. She had come from Spain, but her original point of departure was Cuba. Although she was the daughter of its leader, Fidel Castro, she disagreed violently with her father's politics and had been trying to leave Cuba for years. Once in the United States, she was granted political asylum. This meant that, like other refugees, she entered the country legally, was eligible for federal financial support, and was not counted as part of the yearly quota of immigrants.

That same month, in the darkness of night, a young man shivering in a thin jacket slipped into Texas across the United States-Mexico border. We do not know his name, where he came from, or where he was going. But we do know that he was one of the thousands of Mexicans who enter the United

States every year to look for work. He was an illegal immigrant, subject to deportation if caught by the border patrol.

Both of these people are considered "Hispanics" by the American government. This means that they speak Spanish (or their ancestors did), usually because they come from the Spanish-speaking parts of Latin America. (Another term for this ethnic group is "Latino.") But, as you can see, these two newcomers are very different. They differ in where they came from, how they got here, and what happened to them after they arrived.

Altogether, there are about twenty-two million Hispanics in the United States.[1] This chapter will focus on Mexican Americans, Cuban Americans, and Puerto Ricans, but there are other Hispanic groups as well. They include Dominicans and other peoples from the Caribbean region; Salvadorans and others from Central America; and Colombians and others from South America.

Mexican-American Immigrants

The largest Hispanic group in the United States—about fourteen million—consists of people from Mexico and their descendants.[2] Some Mexicans became Americans in the 1840s, after the United States acquired from Mexico the western lands where they lived. The families of most Mexican Americans, however, came to the United States in the 1900s.

Mexico shares a long border with the United States. For decades there were few restrictions to prevent Mexicans from moving back and forth between their country and the United

States. They could move north to work in the United States, and then return south when they wanted to go home. Many Mexicans were temporary residents, living in the United States for a few months or a few years at a time.

Mexicans tended to move north in great numbers when times were hard in Mexico and when American employers needed workers. For instance, between 1910 and 1930, revolution was disrupting Mexico, and American prosperity was at a high point. One-eighth of the entire Mexican population is said to have moved to the United States during this period.[3] For most of the years between 1942 and 1964, a special program hired Mexican laborers—*braceros*—for temporary work in the United States. Mexicans have been moving north at a high rate in recent years. In the 1980s the yearly average of legal immigrants from Mexico was 97,000.[4] An unknown number come illegally by walking or swimming across the United States-Mexico border. They form a majority of the estimated 100,000 to 200,000 illegal aliens who enter the United States every year.[5]

The majority of Mexican Americans have a mestizo (mixed) background. This means that some of their ancestors were white Europeans and others were Native Americans. A teenager describes his people this way: "If you are Mexican, inside you, around you, you feel the Indian and the Spanish cultures. I am both these cultures."[6] The typical Mexican American has a Spanish name, speaks or understands Spanish, and is a Roman Catholic. At the same time he or she has the brownish skin, black hair, and dark eyes of an Aztec, Maya, or

Like generations of immigrants before them, Hispanic newcomers often work at low-paying jobs because they lack skills or do not speak English. This newly-arrived Mexican boy sells flowers on a busy city street.

other Indian. In the towns of the Southwest and California, where most Mexicans settled, they lived in their own quarter, the *barrio*. They did so partly out of feelings of community and partly because of discrimination by Anglos, since their brown skins aroused racial prejudice. (Anglos is the usual Mexican term for all of those not Mexican.) Illegal immigrants also faced extra burdens. Because they had no legal standing, they could not take action against greedy landlords or cheating employers.

Why Cubans Emigrated

"My father was a political prisoner. He spent nine years in jail in my country. His crime was he didn't like Castro." Jorge, a Cuban American, is explaining why his family moved to the United States. After his father got out of jail, he tried to get a visa, permission to enter the United States legally.

> But it wasn't possible. . . . So he went to work cleaning the sewers, the job the government let him have. . . . In Cuba, the government controls your life . . . . My father decided we would come here illegally.

Jorge's family, after first spending several months in Venezuela, was finally able to settle in Miami.[7]

The Caribbean island of Cuba lies only ninety miles from the U.S. mainland. Cuban immigration, however, was not heavy until the 1960s. It increased then because Fidel Castro, who had overthrown the Cuban government in 1959, set up a Communist dictatorship on the island. Over two hundred fifty five thousand Cubans poured into the United States between 1961 and 1970.[8] The United States made special legal provisions to admit them as political refugees. A second large wave of Cubans came by boat from the Cuban port of Mariel in 1980, when Castro temporarily removed restrictions on leaving the country.

Most of the early immigrants from Cuba were skilled and well educated. They also tended to identify themselves as white. (Black slavery existed in Cuba until the 1880s, and the country has many blacks and people of mixed heritage.) The "Marielitos" included more working people, and more people of black and mixed racial background.

Today there are over one million Americans of Cuban descent in the United States.[9] Over two-thirds of them live in the South, where they are concentrated in Florida. Because of its thousands of Cuban Americans, Miami has the highest proportion of foreign-born residents of an American city.[10] The Miami metropolitan area, once mainly a resort town for the elderly, has become a center of international trade, particularly trade with Latin America.

On the whole Cubans have done well in the United States. Their average income is higher than that of any other Hispanic group.[11] Their success stems partly from their relatively high level of skill and education and partly from the fact that, as political refugees, they received special help from the United States government.

At first most Cubans in the United States thought of themselves as temporary residents. They hoped to return to

Cuba when Castro was overthrown. They were confident that this would happen soon. As time passed, however, Castro remained in power. A younger generation in the United States had less interest in their country of ancestry. Said a Cuban American in Miami: "We Cubans are realists. None of us are going back. . . . But our dream gave us strength when we needed it, and if we can't quite let go, is that really so terrible?"[12]

Puerto Rican Migrants

Like Cuba, Puerto Rico is a large island in the Caribbean Sea. But while Cuba is an independent nation, Puerto Rico is part of the United States. Its inhabitants are United States citizens.

Puerto Rico is not rich, and its standard of living is lower than that of the mainland. In the 1940s, when air travel became common, Puerto Ricans began coming north in great numbers. They could fly to New York City for as little as $50. Today there are over two and a half million Puerto Ricans living on the mainland, mostly in large cities of the East and Midwest.[13] Many Puerto Ricans—probably a majority—represent a mixture of white and black ancestry. Puerto Rican Spanish has a special term, *trigueño*, to designate this mixture, which carries no stigma. In the United States, on the other hand, people are classified as either black or white. People who seem to have any African characteristics are classified as black—and blacks face prejudice and discrimination. This is how one Puerto Rican teenager sees it:

In Puerto Rico there's no distinction between black and brown—you have all sorts of people, you have white, you have black, you have in-between, tan, what have you, and everybody respects everybody. They make no distinction because of color. . . . Over here you have too much prejudice.[14]

Puerto Ricans have faced more than racial discrimination. Many have lacked education and skills. They have had to live in segregated *barrios* and work at low-paying jobs. Since they usually have relatives in Puerto Rico, they have tended to move back and forth, spending a few years on the mainland, returning to the island, and then repeating the journeys.

Hispanics in American Society

The many different groups of Spanish-speaking people in the United States do not usually think of themselves as Hispanic. Instead, they describe themselves as of Mexican, Cuban, Puerto Rican (or whatever) background. Even so, however, they have some things in common.

Many Hispanics view themselves as temporary residents in the United States. This is especially true of Mexicans and Puerto Ricans, who can easily travel back and forth to their homelands. The feeling of impermanence helps explain why so many Hispanics do not become American citizens. Only about 15 percent of the immigrants from Mexico admitted in 1977 had become citizens by 1990. The average rate was 37.4 percent, while the rate for some countries — including the former Soviet Union and most Asian nations — was much higher.[15]

Another sign of loose ties to the United States is the fact that Hispanics tend not to vote even when they are citizens. In the 1988 presidential election, for example, less than 29 percent of eligible Hispanics voted, compared with 57.4 percent of the total population.[16]

Although not all Hispanics may be active in politics, those who are have increased their influence in recent years. Among Mexican Americans, one of the best known spokespeople was a migrant farm worker named Cesar Chavez. He became famous when he led successful strikes against the big farming interests that employed thousands of Mexicans.

In the 1980s the number of Hispanic elected officials increased from fewer than three thousand to more than four thousand.[17] The growing political influence of Mexican Americans was indicated by the elections of Henry Cisneros and Federico Peña to President Clinton's cabinet. Other notable Hispanics in political office have included Herman Badillo, the first Puerto Rican elected to Congress; and Ileana Ros-Lehtinen, the first Cuban American (and first Hispanic woman) elected to Congress.

With the ethnic revival of the 1960s, Hispanics took new pride in their sense of identity. (Mexican Americans called it *La Raza.*) Schools began to teach courses in Hispanic, Latino, or Chicano (another word for "Mexican") studies.

The clearest sign of ethnic pride among Hispanics was the

bilingual (two-language) issue. Beginning in the 1970s, the federal government passed laws to help students whose native language was not English. A high percentage of Hispanics speak Spanish and little or no English. The favored method of helping Spanish-speaking students has been to teach them in both Spanish and English, rather than to give them extra instruction in English alone. It is unclear whether bilingual education is the best way to help students whose native language is not English.[18] But for Hispanics, maintaining their native language is an important symbol of pride in their ethnic heritage.

Many Hispanics share similar attitudes toward the family. In general the father is the boss. Traditionally men work outside the home, while women are homemakers. Males are proud of their strength and masculinity *(machismo)*. Families are close and loyal. As one Puerto Rican girl put it, "To a Puerto Rican, even a bad family is better than no family."[19] Discipline is strict, especially for girls.

Maybe because their homelands are relatively near, Hispanics feel a special closeness to them. Many are conscious of a divided loyalty. A teenager explains:

> *In my future, I dream that I have a good profession and I am married. I have children and I raise them with two languages; always Spanish in the house, English in the street. That's very important. I will tell them how Cuba was and how Cuba is. But I want you to know this: I feel good here in America. This is a very beautiful country. I'm not American, but I feel very proud of America. I think this is my adult mother, America.*[20]

68

7

Native Americans and The Ethnic Experience

Native Americans are a unique people. Their ancestors came to America long before anyone else. Yet not until this century did they formally gain United States citizenship. Native Americans form a small group compared to African Americans or Hispanics (or Americans of German, Irish, or English descent). Yet people all over the world know about them and their history. The government made stronger efforts to force Native Americans into "Anglo-conformity" than it did with any other ethnic group. Even so, they managed to preserve many of their traditions.

According to the census, there are about two million Native Americans in the United States today.[1] About 40 percent live on or near reservations or other special territories set aside for them. The rest live among the general population.[2] Most identify with a tribe (also known as a nation, a people, or an ethnic group). The federal government recognizes about five hundred of these groups.[3] They vary in size from the Navajos of the Southwest, with almost two hundred thousand members, to the Chumash of California, with only around one hundred members.[4]

Christopher Columbus mistakenly called the natives of North America "Indians" because he thought he had landed in the East Indies. Today the term "Native Americans" is widely used.

Background to Conflict

Crossing a land bridge that once linked Siberia and Alaska, the ancestors of today's Native Americans entered North America sometime between twelve thousand and fifty thousand years ago.[5] They were hunters looking for game. Gradually the search of these ancient Americans moved them southward until they had people spread throughout the whole western hemisphere.

In the regions south of what became the United States, the Mayas, Aztecs, and Incas developed advanced civilizations. In our land, Native-American cultures were simpler, but varied. The peoples of the eastern woodlands lived by a combination of hunting and farming. These native groups included the Massachusets and Wampanoags of New England, the Iroquois and Chippewas of the Great Lakes region, and the Creeks and Cherokees of the Southeast. West of the Mississippi lived the buffalo hunters of the Great Plains—the Lakotas (Sioux), Cheyennes, Comanches, and

HARPER'S
NEW MONTHLY MAGAZINE.

No. CCV.—JUNE, 1867.—Vol. XXXV.

THE COURSE OF EMPIRE.

Most Americans of the 1860's, when this engraving was made, saw the westward movement as a triumph of progress and democracy. The train and settlers' wagons in the background symbolize these forces. Native Americans — living in tepees and armed with spears — were viewed as little more than a barrier that could be easily overcome.

others. In the Southwest were the village-dwelling farmers known as the Pueblos and their neighbors, the Navajos.

In the region that became the United States, there were probably about one million Native Americans at the time Europeans first arrived.[6] There was no single culture in this region. For instance, shelters varied from the bark wigwams of the woodlands to the skin tepees of the plains to the adobe dwellings of the Southwest. The people spoke many different languages. But these Native Americans had some things in common. One was their limited technology. They had no horses or other draft animals and therefore no wheeled vehicles. They rarely used metals and did not possess gunpowder. They had no form of written language.

Native Americans in the region that became the United States also had certain attitudes in common. One involved land. They did not believe in individual ownership. Instead they thought of an area as the home of a tribe or band, to be shared by all members. Secondly, Native Americans believed that a supernatural force, or spirit, existed in everything in the universe. They felt themselves to be only one part of nature, trying to live in harmony with it.

The European settlers who first came to North America in the early 1600s were at first few in number. But it was not long before they outnumbered the Native Americans. The Europeans also represented various traditions and spoke different languages. They too had some things in common. Technologically they had the advantage of horses, wheeled vehicles, and metal tools and weapons—including guns. They too shared certain attitudes. One was a strong belief in individual ownership of land. Land was wealth, to be passed down from one generation to the next. Another belief was that people were destined to control the earth for their own benefit. According to the Bible, God had commanded the first humans to fill the world and subdue it and "have dominion over . . . every living thing that moves upon the earth." Finally, Europeans (and their American descendants) shared the same attitude toward Native Americans: They were "savages"—sometimes noble, sometimes ruthless, but always different from, and inferior to, whites.

Given this background, when Native Americans and whites came into contact, conflict was probably inevitable. The whites' superior technology and greater numbers eventually won. But the struggle between Native Americans and whites was a long one. It was a tragic story, filled with misunderstanding, betrayal, war, and conquest. A scholar has written: "What the white man did was terrible. It was wrong. It could not be helped. It cannot be remedied."[7]

Breaking Native-American Resistance: East of the Mississippi

From the beginning the behavior of whites toward Native Americans was contradictory. In some respects the settlers treated tribal groups as if they were independent nations. In negotiating for land, the whites signed treaties and made payments in trade goods such as ironware, guns, and whiskey.

73

On the other hand, if the Native Americans tried to resist and remain on the land, the whites used force.

Some Native Americans fought back. As early as the 1620s, they attacked settlers in Virginia and were defeated. In New England, whites crushed an uprising in the 1670s that was led by a Wampanoag known as King Philip. After their victory, the settlers cut off Philip's head and mounted it on a pole in Plymouth. They sold his widow and son into slavery.

Both Native Americans and whites took advantage of rivalries among their opponents. In the Northeast the Iroquois gained advantages from the English by threatening to side with the French. The Creeks played a similar power game in the Southeast. Whites also played one Native-American group against another—for instance, the Iroquois against the Hurons. Traditional Native-American conflicts were heightened by competition over the fur trade, which could bring handsome profits to the Native-American hunters who supplied white merchants.

When the United States came into being after the Revolutionary War, the federal government continued to make treaties with various Native-American groups. By this time, the region east of the Mississippi River was filling up with whites, steadily pushing Native Americans westward. In the early 1800s, a Shawnee leader named Tecumseh tried to form an alliance of many different tribes. If they acted together, he argued, they could hold onto their land:

Brothers—We all belong to one family; we are all children of the Great Spirit; we walk in the same path . . . we must assist each other to bear our burdens . . . The white men are not friends to the Indians: at first, they only asked for land sufficient for a wigwam; now, nothing will satisfy them but the whole of our hunting grounds, from the rising to the setting sun . . . If you do not unite with us, they will first destroy us, and then you will fall an easy prey to them. They have destroyed many nations of red men because they were not united, because they were not friends to each other.[8]

Tecumseh's campaign failed, however. Tribal groups could not unite with their traditional enemies. Nor could they resist white pressures and gifts. As for Tecumseh, he was killed in battle in 1813.

By the time of Tecumseh's death, the United States had expanded beyond the Mississippi. The Louisiana Purchase, negotiated with France, added a huge area extending all the way to the Rocky Mountains. This region, thought to be a desert unfit for whites, was known as "Indian Country." It could serve, Americans believed, as a permanent home for Native Americans.

Many Native Americans moved to "Indian Country" voluntarily. But some refused to go. In the Southeast, the Creeks, Choctaws, Chickasaws, Cherokees, and Seminoles wanted to remain on land that was theirs by treaty. These groups were called the Five Civilized Tribes because they had settled down like whites and become farmers. The Cherokees even developed their own alphabet.

In 1830 Congress obliged would-be American settlers in the Southeast by passing the Indian Removal Act, which forced the Native Americans off their land. Over the next few years, the Native Americans had to sell their farms at ridiculously low prices. They were then herded westward into a special territory, more or less the same as the present-day state of Oklahoma. So many Cherokees died on the forced march that it has been known ever since as the "Trail of Tears."

Breaking Native-American Resistance: West of the Mississippi

In the 1830s Americans began settling in Texas. Soon afterward, they started moving into the fertile lands of Oregon and California. Wagon trains rumbled across Native-American lands, to be followed soon afterward by transcontinental railroads. Through warfare and treaties, the United States acquired all the land to the Pacific Ocean. White farmers, miners, and ranchers poured into the trans-Mississippi West. Clashes between Native Americans and whites were common.

Beginning in the 1850s, the government adopted a new policy of setting up reservations—specific regions where Native Americans had to live. There they would own the land in common and receive supplies of food and clothing until they could support themselves. One aim of this policy was to end armed conflict. The other was to open new areas for white settlement. At first reservation lands were enormous, but they were gradually reduced in size.

Few Native Americans were happy to "come in" to reservations. A Kiowa chief named Satanta spoke for many when he told the whites: "I have heard that you intend to settle us on a reservation near the mountains. I don't want to settle. I love to roam over the prairies. There I feel free and happy, but when we settle down we grow pale and die."[9]

The Native Americans knew that they were outnumbered. "The white men are like the locusts," one Sioux put it. "Kill one, kill two, kill ten, and ten times ten will come to kill you."[10] In any case, the old way of life was impossible because the buffalo were disappearing. White "sportsmen"—many shooting from trains—were slaughtering thousands of the animals for their hides. In 1850 the herds had numbered some twenty million. In 1889 an official count revealed a total of 551.[11]

Tragic episodes of violence characterized relations between Native Americans and whites in the late 1800s. At Sand Creek, Colorado, 200 Cheyennes—mostly women and children—were massacred after they had agreed to "come in" to a reservation. In revenge Sioux warriors killed innocent farmers and ranchers. In 1876 thousands of Sioux, Cheyennes, and Arapahoes camped along the Little Bighorn River of Montana. Led by Tatanka Yotanka (Sitting Bull) and Tashunka Witko (Crazy Horse), they defied a government order to leave the open range. When army forces advanced on them, they wiped out an entire detachment of 225 troops led by General George Custer.[12] After "Custer's Last Stand," the army relentlessly pursued any bands that disobeyed government orders. The last armed resistance, that of the Apaches, was crushed when their leader, Geronimo, surrendered in 1886 in Mexico.

"Kill the Indian and Save the Man"

By 1880 almost all Native Americans were on reservations. They were poor and discouraged. Their numbers had been reduced to about two-hundred seventy five thousand.[13] The decline in population was due in part to warfare and the shocks of being uprooted. Another factor was disease. Over the years, thousands of Native Americans had died from unfamiliar diseases brought from overseas, among them measles, smallpox, and tuberculosis. It was common, in fact, to refer to Native Americans as "vanishing Americans."

A lot of people, especially land-hungry westerners, thought that if Native Americans did die out, it would be a good solution. They agreed with General Philip Sheridan. He was famous for remarking to a Cheyenne who claimed to be a "good Indian" that "the only good Indians I ever saw were dead."[14] Many other Americans, however, took a more humane view. They were people such as Helen Hunt Jackson. In her book, *A Century of Dishonor* (published in 1881), she attacked the injustice and betrayals that had reduced the Native Americans to their sorry state.

As reformers saw it, isolating Native Americans on reservations and supporting them with handouts was no solution.

Instead, they should be completely assimilated into American society. The United States owed the Native Americans a debt, wrote one expert. "The major portion of that debt can be paid only by giving to the Indians Anglo-Saxon civilization, that they may also have prosperity and happiness under the new civilization of this continent."[15]

Native American cultures had already been affected by "white" ways. Buffalo hunters of the Great Plains had been entirely dependent on the horse, which had not existed in North America until introduced by the Spanish. The Navajos of the Southwest lived by herding sheep, another animal brought to the New World by Europeans. Most Native Americans learned English, and many adopted some form of Christianity.

On the other hand, many continued to speak their native language among themselves. They liked to wear traditional clothing, which included buckskin garments, feather decorations, and long hair and jewelry for both sexes. They maintained ancient religious rituals, often while practicing Christianity as well. Many men had more than one wife. Tribal organization remained strong, and decisions were made by consensus—with everyone agreeing—rather than by majority vote.

Assimilation, to the reformers, meant that Native Americans had to abandon their own cultures and become "Americans." (The authorities wanted the same objective for immigrants, but they had more control over Native Americans.) The reformers' goal was to "kill the Indian and save the man." They planned to achieve it through a three-part program of education, individual ownership of land, and citizenship.

Education of young Native Americans, it was believed, should occur at boarding schools, far away from the reservations. The most famous school was Carlisle, in Pennsylvania, which opened in 1879. At schools like this, youths had to discard their native clothes and names, have their hair cut short, stop speaking their native languages, and study the same subjects taught in public schools. The experience of Sun Elk, a boy from Taos pueblo in New Mexico, was typical. He spent seven years at Carlisle.

> *They told us that Indian ways were bad. They said we must get civilized. I remember that word too. It means "be like the white man." I am willing to be like the white man, but I did not believe Indian ways were wrong. But they kept teaching us for seven years. . . . And so after a while we also began to say Indians were bad.*

When Sun Elk finally returned to New Mexico, his people shunned him. "He cannot even speak our language," they said, "and he has a strange smell. He is not one of us." Only after Sun Elk had married an Indian girl did he regain his place in the pueblo. Then, as he put it, he "became an Indian again."[16]

As for individual land ownership, reformers were convinced that Native Americans could become full-fledged members of society only by farming their own plots. The Native American, one official said, "will be a vagabond and a pauper so long as he is not an individual proprietor and possessor."[17]

In 1887 Congress passed the Dawes Act. This law put an end to tribes as legal bodies, and awarded each family 160 acres. The leftover land could be sold, and the plots themselves could be sold after twenty-five years. At this time each owner would also become a citizen.

The campaign to assimilate Native Americans was a failure. Most Native Americans did not want to adopt mainstream culture, but instead kept to their old traditions. As Sitting Bull said, "If the Great Spirit had desired me to be a white man he would have made me so in the first place."[18]

As for farming on individual plots, few Native Americans had the skills or desire to be farmers. In any case much of the land was poor, and the acreage was too small for efficient farming in the West. While tribal groups had to sell their land, individual owners often chose to do the same thing. Between 1887 and 1934, when the Dawes Act was abolished, Native-American holdings declined from 138 million to 52 million acres.[19] Instead of becoming independent, Native Americans had to rely more and more on government aid. In these circumstances, citizenship made little difference. Although many had gained the right earlier, a law of 1924 made all Native Americans citizens.

Gaining the Right To Be Different

The Indian Reorganization Act of 1934 — the same law that ended individual land allotments — slowed down the process

This "before" picture shows a Navajo youth in 1882, when he arrived in Pennsylvania to attend the Carlisle boarding school.

This "after" picture shows the same young Navajo in 1885, after three years at Carlisle. The school distributed pictures like this to show how well its students were being assimilated into the American way of life.

of forced "Anglo-conformity." It allowed land ownership in common and government by tribal organizations. The law also encouraged Native Americans to preserve some of their cultural traditions.

The Native-American population began to increase. Some tribes profited by exploiting oil and other minerals found on their reservations. But many problems remained. Most Native Americans lived in poverty. Their life expectancy was below the average for Americans as a whole. And assimilation was still the basic goal of the United States policy toward Native Americans. During the 1950s the government advocated "relocation" and "termination"—moving Native Americans off reservations and then closing them. This policy, which met with little success, was soon abandoned.

Native Americans benefited from a new approach, "self-determination without termination," announced in 1970. By this time Native Americans (like African Americans and Hispanics) were profiting from the ethnic revival of the 1960s. They formed such organizations as the American Indian Movement, dedicated to strengthening "red power." Newly militant, many tribes sued the government, frequently winning land and water rights, as well as compensation for broken treaties. Beginning in the 1980s, dozens of tribes added to their revenues by opening gambling casinos on their reservations. (These operations were tax-free.)

Native Americans found that the general population was more tolerant of, and even curious about, their customs. Other Americans were interested not only in Native-American arts and crafts, but also in such traditions as their reverence for nature. Ironically, many Native Americans themselves had to attend large gatherings—powwows—to learn about the customs of their ancestors.

One sign of acceptance was a surge in the Native-American population, which apparently tripled between 1960 and 1990.[20] The growth resulted not from a high birthrate, but from the increased willingness of Americans to admit their Native American ancestry. "There were many people who were ashamed of their Indian past, so they hid it," said a Cherokee sociologist. "But a lot of people who went the assimilationist route have come back."

As an ethnic group, Native Americans have a unique place. In many respects their lives have been shaped by the culture of the American mainstream. At the same time, however, they have stubbornly maintained their own separate identity. Theirs has been a difficult course between extremes, as these observers note:

> *Had the tribes abandoned their old ways and wholeheartedly adopted the new institutions of the intruders, we would have no identifiable Indians today. On the other hand, if they had absolutely resisted any changes, we most probably would not have Indians today either.*[21]

8

Where Do We Go from Here?

It was a bright fall weekend in 1990. With bands, flags, dancing, songs, and speeches, Americans held a two-day celebration at Ellis Island in New York Harbor. The red-brick buildings of Ellis Island, a major gateway to America, had processed more than twelve million immigrants between 1892 and 1924.[1] After being closed, the buildings had fallen into disrepair. Now refurbished, they were reopening as a museum honoring the immigrant experience.

Over the centuries the United States has taken in 50,000,000 immigrants.[2] "The long line of people waiting to get in forms this country's central experience," wrote a Frenchman-turned-American in the 1970s. "It sets America apart from the rest of the world in its willingness to accept and its capacity to absorb outsiders in large numbers."[3] How have this acceptance and this absorption actually worked?

The first chapter of this book ended with three questions:

Has our country been a melting pot? Is it one now? Should it be? Later chapters explained that the melting-pot concept was a metaphor for processes of acculturation and assimilation— processes that have also been compared with an orchestra, a salad bowl, a mosaic, and so on. As you read this concluding chapter, look for your answers to the three initial questions. You may also want to think about which metaphor you think is most accurate. (This chapter uses the term "melting pot" for simplicity's sake.)

Ethnic Identity

Has the United States been a melting pot? One way to answer this question is to see how the population as a whole views itself. As you've read, Americans began to develop a new attitude toward ethnic groups in the late 1960s. The 1980 census reflected the growing interest in ethnicity. For the first time the Census Bureau asked Americans to describe their "ancestry group" (the term preferred by the bureau), no matter how many generations they had been in the United States. (In earlier censuses, this question was asked only of the first- or second-generation respondents.) The form gave a few examples, including "Italian," "Jamaican," "Korean," and "Polish." It also noted that "a religious group should not be reported as a person's ancestry."

The table on page 88 summarizes some of the information on ethnic groups gathered by the 1990 census.[4] About 90 percent of Americans responded to the question. As you can see, Germany, Ireland, and England led all other countries

Most Frequently Reported
Ancestry Groups – 1990 Census

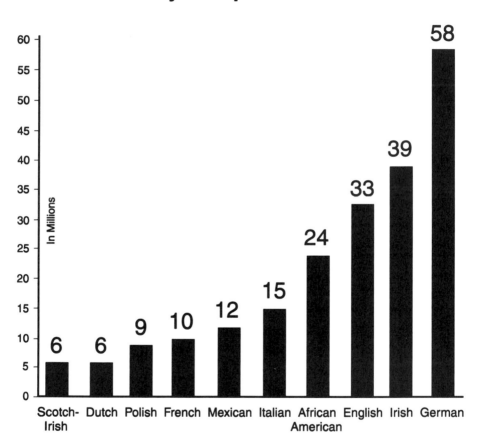

According to the 1990 federal census, more Americans claimed German ancestry than any other.

specified by the respondents. Among non-European ancestors, those from Africa and Mexico were mentioned most frequently. Answers to the question about ancestry reveal interesting information about American identity. A total of 30 percent of respondents gave two ancestry groups. (These were counted separately, which is why the total number of responses was greater than the total population.) If respondents describe their ancestry as, say, both Polish and Italian, they are indicating that somewhere in their past a Polish ancestor married an Italian ancestor. Intermarriage is one sure sign of assimilation—of the melting pot at work. Another sign is the number of people who answered "American" or "United States" when questioned about their nationality. This total, over thirteen million, amounts to about 5 percent of the population.

The census, however, is only one indicator of American ethnicity. Surveys are another. One survey was conducted recently among the descendants of European immigrants in the region around Albany, New York. Responses from several hundred people of European descent revealed that only very small percentages of them spoke the language of their ethnic group, belonged to ethnic social clubs, taught their children ethnic traditions, or even ate ethnic foods on a daily basis.[5] Another survey, conducted in California and Pennsylvania, indicated that Americans choose how ethnic to be, and—when they represent mixtures—which ethnicity, if any, to stress.[6]

Personal expression is yet another way in which Americans indicate their feelings about identity. Some people are fascinated by their heritage, and spend years researching family histories. One of the most celebrated searches was carried out by the African-American writer Alex Haley. Using family memories and a few African words as clues, Haley spent twelve years and traveled half a million miles in search of the African ancestors on his mother's side. He found them in Gambia. The book that resulted—*Roots*, published in 1976—and the television series based on it reached an audience of millions. It is interesting to note, by the way, that if Haley had investigated his father's ancestry instead of his mother's, he would have ended up in Ireland rather than Africa.

Langston Hughes was also interested in his African heritage. When he asked himself about his African roots, he answered that "I did not feel the rhythms of the primitive surging through me. I was only an American Negro—but I was not Africa. I was Chicago and Kansas City and Broadway and Harlem." At the same time, Hughes admitted, he felt that he could hear a song of Africa through "some vast mist of race."[7]

A similar attitude was that of a Harvard professor named Thomas Pettigrew. When he and his Scottish immigrant mother visited Inverness, the town of her birth, he later wrote: "I learned how different I really was from my Scots relatives, whom I liked very much. In short, though proud to be of Scottish origin, what I really found was that my roots are in America, that I am disgustingly American."[8]

Many people are simply indifferent to their ethnicity.

(Remember that 10 percent of those surveyed in the 1990 census did not answer the question about ancestry.) As one scholar has written, "You may not be able to change your grandparents but you can forget them—and many Americans have."[9]

Barbara Ehrenreich, a writer, was asked by a friend what her ethnic background was. After blurting out "none," Ehrenreich had second thoughts.

> *Well, not "none," I backtracked. Scottish, English, Irish—that was something, I supposed. Too much Irish to qualify as a WASP; too much of the hated English to warrant a "Kiss Me, I'm Irish" button; plus there are a number of dead ends in the family tree due to adoptions, missing records, failing memories and the like. I was blushing by this time. Did "none" mean I was rejecting my heritage out of Anglo-Celtic self-hate? Or was I revealing a hidden ethnic chauvinism in which the Britannically derived serve as a kind of neutral standard compared with the ethnic "others"?*

Ehrenreich comments on the ethnic consciousness of the 1960s and 1970s, especially among minorities, as a time when "I just sank back ever deeper into my seat."

> *All this excitement over ethnicity stemmed, I uneasily sensed, from a past in which their ancestors had been trampled upon by my ancestors, or at least by people who looked very much like them. In addition, it had begun to seem almost un-American not to have some sort of hyphen at hand, linking one to more venerable times and locales.*

Finally, however, Ehrenreich concludes that:

> *the truth is, I was raised with none. . . . We are the kind*
> *of people . . . who do not believe, who do not carry on*
> *traditions, who do not do things just because someone has*
> *done them before. . . . What was the past, as our*
> *forebears knew it? Nothing but poverty, superstition, and*
> *grief.*[10]

Reactions of Newcomers

Is the United States a melting pot today? Let's look at how recent immigrants view themselves and the country in which they live.

In the 1990s the number of immigrants has averaged almost one and a half million every year.[11] About 8 percent of today's population was born in another country.[12] These totals are similar to those from the peak years of immigration early in the 1900s. But the nature of today's immigration is very different. In 1910, 88 percent of the immigrants came from Europe, with only 2 percent from Asia and 8 percent from the western hemisphere.[13] In 1990, only 7 percent of immigrants came from Europe, whereas 22 percent came from Asia and 62 percent from the western hemisphere.[14]

The shift in geography has also meant a racial shift. In 1910, 88 percent of Americans were white and 12 percent nonwhite.[15] In 1990, 80 percent of Americans were white and 20 percent nonwhite or Hispanic.[16] (As you've read, many Hispanics are nonwhite.) The two fastest-growing segments of our population are Hispanics and Asians. According to some estimates, the "average" American by the year 2056—when someone born today will be sixty-six years old—will trace her or his descent not to Europe but to Africa, Asia, the Hispanic world, or the Pacific Islands.[17] "This is the dawning of the first universal nation," comments one observer. "It's going to cause some turmoil, but on balance it's an incredibly poetic fact."[18]

The changing nature of immigration concerns many Americans because the United States has traditionally been less than hospitable to nonwhites. And nonwhites, in turn, have felt less than committed to their adopted country. (Remember, for example, Pany Lowe in Chapter Four.)

For both nonwhite and white immigrants, however, it seems safe to say that the processes of acculturation and assimilation continue to work more or less as they did earlier. Look at language, for example. Many newcomers, of course, speak a language other than English. The 1990 census asked foreign-born persons speaking another language to indicate if they did not speak English "very well." Of foreigners born in Mexico, 73 percent admitted that they were not fluent in English; 74 percent of those of Chinese origin answered similarly.[19] It seems clear, though, that foreigners want to learn English. For instance, a poll conducted in Houston in 1990 found that 87 percent of all Hispanics believed that it was their "duty to learn English."[20] A recent Russian immigrant cautioned his fellow immigrants: "You should learn English. Going to other Russians will not help very much. What they call networking works very fine, but you should do it in

English. If you want to eat, you have to speak."[21] It also seems clear that later generations of today's immigrants will be less fluent in the language of their ancestors. The publisher of two Spanish-language periodicals in the United States spoke about his community:

> *I see new immigrants moving in, then opening up stores, taking over stores originally owned by Italians. Those immigrant kids will then move up the ladder. It's the same cycle. Ideally, in the long run, this paper will turn English.*[22]

Intermarriage is another indicator of assimilation. To take just one example, Japanese Americans marry non-Japanese Americans about 65 percent of the time. Since 1981 the number of babies born in the United States with one Japanese-American and one white parent has exceeded the number with two Japanese-American parents.[23]

The difficulties of immigrating to a foreign country should not be underestimated. An Ibo woman from Nigeria writes of herself and other women from traditional societies.

> *We straddle two cultures, cultures that are often in opposition. Mainstream America, the culture we embrace in our professional lives, dictates that we be assertive and independent—like men. Our traditional culture, dictated by religion and years of socialization, demands that we be docile and content in our roles as mothers and wives—careers or not.*[24]

And a Vietnamese boy advises fellow students at an

international high school: "America may be your home for the rest of your life, but don't forget where you came from. . . . Don't forget your past, no matter how good or bad it was."[25]

A young Thai woman reached this optimistic conclusion, mathematically impossible as it may sound:

> *I'm 100% American and 100% Asian. A lot of Asian Americans feel forced to choose between the two, which is a message they get from their parents. But I've worked hard to create a cultural hybrid for myself.*[26]

The Case for Diversity

Should the United States be a melting pot? Many people say no. (They are often called multiculturalists.) They argue that our various ethnicities are just as important, if not more important, than any heritage we may share with our fellow Americans.

One argument of multiculturalists is that knowledge of our roots is a good thing. According to Michael Novak:

> *Diversity is a better model [than unity] for America, for the self, and indeed for the human race upon this planet. . . . When ethnic cultures and family values are weakened in the pressures of the melting pot, is anything substituted except . . . success and the pursuit of loneliness?*[27]

Asserting our differences, say multiculturalists, is also necessary in order to reverse the wrongs of the past. For too long, Americanism, as Anglo-conformity, tried to press thousands

As American as apple pie.

And enchiladas.

And moo goo gai pan.

And couscous.

And ratatouille.

And gyros.

And panggang bungkus.

And fettucine.

And wiener schnitzel.

Today there's more cultural variety on America's plate than ever before. With many more immigrants coming from the Far East, Latin America, and Africa, we're no longer the traditional melting pot of European cultures, but are becoming the world's first truly international nation. Read about it in this special 53rd issue of TIME. *If it's important to you, you'll find it in TIME.*

On sale Nov. 8.

Those who support multiculturalism find us, as Americans, to be the sum of all of our different nationalities. This advertisement for a special issue of *Time* magazine points out the many international foods that immigrants have brought to this country.

of immigrants into the same mold. The only true "Americans," it seemed, were WASPs. Generations of Irish, Germans, Italians, Jews, and others were made to feel that there was something shameful in the heritage they brought with them from Europe. And it was worse for people of color—blacks, Hispanics, Asians, and Native Americans. There seemed to be no room at all for them in the melting pot.

Many multiculturalists believe that our society has to make up for decades of belittling or ignoring ethnicity. Doing so will build self-esteem, especially among minorities. Schools, which were in the forefront of Americanism, should be in the forefront of the new emphasis on diversity. For instance, classes in American history should describe westward expansion from the point of view of Native Americans as well as white settlers. If necessary schools should help students who want to know more about their own past. A Navajo girl wrote this about her experience:

> *My grandmom was taught how to pray in Navajo ways when she was just a little girl. But I was taught how to pray in white ways. Now I have to take Navajo history in class, to learn all my old people's ways. My grandfather once knew all about the sacred mountains. But now he is gone.*[28]

The Case for Unity

Should the United States be a melting pot? Many answer yes. (They are often called traditionalists.) While they strongly oppose the forced assimilation that has given the melting pot a bad name, they believe that Americans should emphasize how they are alike, not how they differ. Doing so is necessary because Americans are so diverse.

America was built on certain ideals, including tolerance, democratic government, and the freedoms outlined in the Bill of Rights. Traditionalists argue that these form a common bond—patriotism—that can, and should, link us all. Early European settlers brought these ideals with them. Over the centuries they were extended (in a process still unfinished) to minorities and women. Today's immigrants know what these ideals are. They presumably believe in them too or they would not come here.

Many who favor multiculturalism claim that the American past has little relevance for many ethnic groups. Clinton government official Donna Shalala commented, "My grandparents came from Lebanon. I don't identify with the Pilgrims on a personal level."[29] Traditionalists disagree. The writer Richard Rodriguez, whose parents came from Mexico, has written:

> *I needed to learn the names of British kings and dissident Protestants, because they were the beginning of us. I read the writings of eighteenth-century white men who powdered their wigs and kept slaves, because these were the men who shaped the country that shaped my life.*[30]

It is not the business of schools, traditionalists say, to lead "ethnic cheerleading." If an ethnic heritage is strong enough, it will be passed on by such traditional means as the family.

What about the argument that Americanism and appeals

to patriotism have been oppressive and damaging? A teacher responds:

> *There is no incompatibility between respect for cultural differences and American patriotism. Like every other country, ours has a lot to be proud of and a lot to be ashamed of. But a nation cannot reform itself unless it takes pride in itself—unless it has an identity, rejoices in it, reflects upon it and tries to live up to it. Such pride sometimes takes the form of arrogant, bellicose [warlike] nationalism. But it often takes the form of a yearning to live up to the nation's professed ideals.*[31]

It may not be possible to reach a compromise between these two arguments. But Americans on both sides might consider, and even accept, a revised Pledge of Allegiance suggested by a law professor named George Fletcher:

> *I pledge allegiance to the flag of the United States of America and to the Republic for which it stands, one nation, united in our diversity, committed to liberty and justice for all.*[32]

99

Chapter Notes

Chapter 1
1. New York City Board of Education, 1994 statistics.

Chapter 2
1. Joan Morrison and Charlotte Fox Zabusky, eds., *American Mosaic: The Immigrant Experience in the Words of Those Who Lived It* (New York: E.P. Dutton, 1980), p. 295.

2. See Lawrence Wright, "One Drop of Blood," *New Yorker*, July 25, 1994.

3. Eddy L. Harris, *Native Stranger: A Black American's Journey into the Heart of Africa* (New York: Simon & Schuster, 1992), p. 106.

4. Jodi Padnick, "What Being Jewish Means to Me," advertisement for The American Jewish Committee, *The New York Times*, November 21, 1993, section 4, p. 17.

5. Stephen Thernstrom, ed., *Harvard Encyclopedia of American Ethnic Groups* (Cambridge, Mass.: Harvard University Press, 1980).

6. Definitions of ethnic groups vary. While the *Harvard Encyclopedia of Ethnic Groups* recognizes Jews as an American ethnic group, the U.S. Census Bureau does not.

7. "Muslim Women Bridging Culture Gap," *The New York Times*, November 8, 1993, p. B9.

8. Louis Adamic, *My America, 1928-1938* (New York: Harper & Brothers, 1938), p. 223.

Chapter 3
1. U.S. Census Bureau, *Statistical Abstract of the United States: 1992*, 112th ed. (Washington, D.C.: 1992), p. 8.

2. Phillip Viereck, ed., *The New Land* (New York: John Day Co., 1967), p. 170.

3. U.S. Census Bureau, *Historical Statistics of the United States: Colonial Times to 1970* (Washington, D.C.: 1975), p. 1168.

4. Arthur Mann, *The One and the Many: Reflections on the American Identity* (Chicago: University of Chicago Press, 1979), p. 49.

5. *Historical Statistics*, p. 106.

6. Ibid.

7. Ibid.

8. Robert Ernst, *Immigrant Life in New York City: 1825-1863* (New York: Octagon, 1979), p. 67.

9. *Historical Statistics*, p. 105.

10. Milton M. Gordon, *Assimilation in American Life: The Role of Race, Religion, and National Origins* (New York: Oxford University Press, 1964), p. 101.

11. Arthur M. Schlesinger, Jr., *The Disuniting of America* (New York: W.W. Norton, 1992), p. 24.

12. Ibid.

13. Ibid. p. 25.

14. Quoted in John Higham, *Strangers in the Land: Patterns of American Nativism, 1860-1925* (New York: Atheneum, 1963), p. 106.

15. Kerby A. Miller, *Emigrants and Exiles: Ireland and the Irish Exodus to North America* (New York: Oxford University Press, 1985), p. 511.

16. Kathleen Neils Conzen, "Ethnicity as Festive Culture: Nineteenth-Century German America on Parade," in Werner Sollors, ed., *The Invention of Ethnicity* (New York: Oxford University Press, 1989), p. 51.

17. Irving Howe, *World of Our Fathers* (New York: Simon & Schuster, 1976), p. 128.

18. Israel Zangwill, *The Melting-Pot* (New York: Arno Press, 1975), pp. 184-185.

19. There is no Anglo-Saxon race, but the word *race* was commonly used at this time for nationalities and ethnic groups.

20. John Higham, *Send These to Me: Immigrants in Urban America* (Baltimore: Johns Hopkins, rev. ed., 1984), p. 41.

21. *Historical Statistics*, p. 105.

Chapter 4

1. Donald Dale Jackson, " 'Behave Like Your Actions Reflect on All Chinese,' " *Smithsonian*, Vol. 21, (February, 1991), p. 120.

2. Kerby A. Miller, *Emigrants and Exiles: Ireland and the Irish Exodus to North America* (New York: Oxford University Press, 1985), p. 319.

3. Oscar Handlin, *Readings in American History* (New York: Knopf, 1957), p. 421.

4. Lawrence H. Fuchs, *The American Kaleidoscope: Race, Ethnicity, and the Civic Future* (Hanover, N.H.: University Press of New England, 1990), p. 65.

5. Milton M. Gordon, *Assimilation in American Life: The Role of Race, Religion, and National Origins* (New York: Oxford University Press, 1964), p. 101.

6. Irving Howe, *World of Our Fathers* (New York: Simon & Schuster, 1976), p. 234.

7. Louis Adamic, *My America, 1928-1938* (New York: Harper & Brothers, 1938), p. 248.

8. "The Transformation of the Statue of Liberty," in John Higham, *Send These to Me: Immigrants in Urban America* (Baltimore: Johns Hopkins, rev. ed., 1984), pp. 71-80.

9. See Philip Gleason, "American Identity and Americanization," in Stephen Thernstrom, ed. *Harvard Encyclopedia of American Ethnic Groups* (Cambridge, Mass.: Harvard University Press, 1980), pp. 31-58.

10. Nathan Glazer and Daniel Patrick Moynihan, *Beyond the Melting Pot: The Negroes, Puerto Ricans, Jews, Italians, and Irish of New York City* (Cambridge, Mass.: M.I.T. Press, 1963), p. v.

11. Michael Novak, *The Rise of the Unmeltable Ethnics: Politics and Culture in the Seventies* (New York: Macmillan, 1972); Peter Schrag, *The Decline of the WASP* (New York: Simon & Schuster, 1971).

12. Arthur Mann, *The One and the Many: Reflections on the American Identity* (Chicago: University of Chicago Press, 1979), p. 36.

13. Ibid., p. 37.

14. Horace M. Kallen, *Culture and Democracy in the United States: Studies in the Group Psychology of the American Peoples* (New York: Boni and Liveright, 1924), pp. 124-125.

15. Fuchs, p. 276.

Chapter 5

1. Langston Hughes, *Selected Poems of Langston Hughes* (New York: Knopf, 1970), p. 275.

2. U.S. Census Bureau, *Statistical Abstract of the United States: 1992*, 112th ed. (Washington, D.C.: 1992), p. 17.

3. Philip D. Curtin, *The Atlantic Slave Trade: A Census* (Madison, Wis.: University of Wisconsin Press, 1969), p. 268.

4. U.S. Census Bureau, *Historical Statistics of the United States: Colonial Times to 1970* (Washington, D.C.: 1975), p. 14.

5. Stuart Berg Flexner, *I Hear America Talking: An Illustrated Treasury of American Words and Phrases* (New York: Van Nostrand, 1976), pp. 33-34.

6. *Historical Statistics*, p. 18.

7. Herbert Aptheker, ed., *A Documentary History of the Negro People in the United States* (New York: Citadel, 1968), Vol. I, p. 771.

8. John Hope Franklin, *From Slavery to Freedom: A History of Negro Americans*, 5th ed., (New York: Knopf, 1980), pp. 221-224.

9. Leslie H. Fishel and Benjamin Quarles, eds., *The Negro American: A Documentary History* (Glenview, Ill.: Scott, Foresman, 1967), p. 343.

10. *Historical Statistics*, pp. 12, 22.

11. Franklin, p. 355.

12. Fishel and Quarles, p. 534.

13. Stephen Thernstrom, ed. *Harvard Encyclopedia of American Ethnic Groups* (Cambridge, Mass.: Harvard University Press, 1980), p. 21.

14. George Breitman, ed., *Malcolm X Speaks* (New York: Pathfinder, 1989), pp. 12, 20.

15. Those who preferred this term believed that it would give black people a greater sense of their history. However, surveys conducted in 1991 indicated that a majority of black Americans preferred "black" to "African American."

16. Arthur Mann, *The One and the Many: Reflections on the American Identity* (Chicago: University of Chicago Press, 1979), p. 174.

17. Lawrence H. Fuchs, *The American Kaleidoscope: Race, Ethnicity, and the Civic Future* (Hanover, N.H.: University Press of New England, 1990), p. 204.

Chapter 6

1. U.S. Census Bureau, *Persons of Hispanic Origin in the United States* (Washington, D.C.: 1993), p. 1.

2. Ibid., p. 5.

3. Alfredo Mirande, *The Chicano Experience: An Alternative*

Perspective (Notre Dame, Ind.: University of Notre Dame Press, 1985), p. 49.

4. U.S. Census Bureau, *Statistical Abstract of the United States: 1992*, 112th ed. (Washington, D.C.: 1992), p. 11.

5. David M. Reimers, *Still the Golden Door: The Third World Comes to America*, 2nd ed., (New York: Columbia University Press, 1992), p. 262.

6. Janet Bode, *New Kids on the Block: Oral Histories of Immigrant Teens* (New York: Franklin Watts, 1989), p. 72.

7. Ibid., pp. 46, 50.

8. *Statistical Abstract 1992*, p. 11.

9. *Persons of Hispanic Origin in the United States*, p. 7.

10. Lawrence H. Fuchs, *The American Kaleidoscope: Race, Ethnicity, and the Civic Future* (Hanover, N.H.: University Press of New England, 1990), p. 299.

11. Rodolfo O. de la Garza et al., *Latino Voices: Mexican, Puerto Rican, and Cuban Perspectives on American Politics* (Boulder, Colo.: Westview Press, 1992), p. 28.

12. David Rieff, *The Exile: Cuba in the Heart of Miami* (New York: Simon & Schuster, 1993), p. 188.

13. *Persons of Hispanic Origin in the United States*, p. 6.

14. Paulette Cooper, ed., *Growing Up Puerto Rican* (New York: New American Library, 1972), p. 122.

15. *1991 Statistical Yearbook of the Immigration and Naturalization Service* (Washington, D.C.: 1992), p. 120.

16. *Statistical Abstract 1992*, p. 269.

17. Ibid., p. 268.

18. Thomas Weyr, *Hispanic U.S.A.: Breaking the Melting Pot* (New York: Harper & Row, 1988), pp. 57-75.

19. Cooper, p. 118.

20. Bode, p. 51.

Chapter 7

1. U.S. Census Bureau, *Statistical Abstract of the United States: 1992*, 112th ed. (Washington, D.C.: 1992), p. 17. Population totals for Native Americans vary widely. The U.S. Census Bureau uses self-identification, while various tribes have differing standards. For membership, some tribes require applicants to prove that they are at

least half Native American. Others accept as little as two-thousandths of Native-American ancestry.

2. Ibid., p. 40.

3. Barry T. Klein, *Reference Encyclopedia of the American Indian* (West Nyack, N.Y.: Todd Publications, 1993) p. i.

4. Ibid., p. 29.

5. A.J. Jaffe, *The First Immigrants from Asia: A Population History of the North American Indians* (New York: Plenum Press, 1992), p. 37.

6. Ibid., p. 107.

7. Brian W. Dippie, *The Vanishing American: White Attitudes and U.S. Indian Policy* (Fort Hays, Kans.: University Press of Kansas, 1982), p. 351.

8. Peter Nabokov, ed., *Native American Testimony: A Chronicle of Indian-White Relations from Prophecy to the Present, 1492-1992* (New York: Viking Penguin, 1991), pp. 96-97.

9. Virginia Irving Armstrong, comp., *I Have Spoken: American History Through the Voices of the Indians* (Chicago: Swallow Press, 1971), p. 86.

10. Ibid., p. 80.

11. Paula Angle Franklin, *Indians of North America: The Eight Culture Areas and How Their Inhabitants Lived Before the Coming of the Whites* (New York: David McKay, 1979), p. 105.

12. Total casualties for both Sand Creek and the Little Bighorn from William C. Sturtevant, ed., *Handbook of North American Indians*, Vol. 4, *History of Indian-White Relations* (Washington, D.C.: Smithsonian Institution, 1988), pp. 168, 176.

13. Jaffe, p. 113.

14. *Bartlett's Familiar Quotations*, 16th ed., (Boston: Little, Brown, 1992), p. 516.

15. Frederick E. Hoxie, *A Final Promise: The Campaign to Assimilate the Indians, 1880-1928* (Lincoln, Nebr.: University of Nebraska Press, 1984), p. 24.

16. Nabokov, pp. 222-224.

17. Dippie, p. 109.

18. Armstrong, p. 112.

19. Herman J. Viola, *After Columbus: The Smithsonian Chronicle of the North American Indians* (Washington, D.C.: Smithsonian Books, 1990), p. 216.

20. Dirk Johnson, "Census Finds Many Claiming New Identity: Indian," *The New York Times*, March 5, 1991, p. A16.

21. Vine Deloria, Jr. and Clifford M. Lytle, *American Indians, American Justice* (Austin, Tex.: University of Texas Press, 1983), p. xi.

Chapter 8

1. Sara Rimer, "Where the World Was New: Immigrants Recall Ellis Island," *The New York Times*, September 9, 1990, section 1, p. 36.

2. Michael D'Innocenzo and Josef P. Sirefman, eds., *Immigration and Ethnicity: American Society — "Melting Pot" or "Salad Bowl"?* (Westport, Conn.: Greenwood Press, 1992), p. ix.

3. Ted Morgan, *On Becoming American* (Boston: Houghton Mifflin, 1978), p. 99.

4. U.S. Census Bureau, *Detailed Ancestry Groups for States* (Washington, D.C.: 1992), pp. III-1, III-4. The question about ancestry — along with many others — is asked only on the long form of the census, which goes to about one-sixth of the households in the United States. From this sample, the Census Bureau infers totals for the entire population.

5. Richard D. Alba, *Ethnic Identity: The Transformation of White America* (New Haven, Conn.: Yale University Press, 1990).

6. Mary C. Waters, *Ethnic Options: Choosing Identities in America* (Berkeley, Calif.: University of California Press, 1990).

7. Ronald Takaki, *A Different Mirror: The History of Multicultural America* (Boston: Little, Brown, 1993), p. 360.

8. Arthur Mann, *The One and the Many: Reflections on the American Identity* (Chicago: University of Chicago Press, 1979), p. 41.

9. Stephen Thernstrom, ed. *Harvard Encyclopedia of American Ethnic Groups* (Cambridge, Mass.: Harvard University Press, 1980), p. vii.

10. Barbara Ehrenreich, "Cultural Baggage," *The New York Times Magazine*, April 5, 1992, pp. 6, 17-18.

11. Immigration and Naturalization Service.

12. U.S. Census Bureau, *Statistical Abstract of the United States: 1992*, 112th ed. (Washington, D.C.: 1992), p. 42.

13. U.S. Census Bureau, *Historical Statistics of the United States: Colonial Times to 1970* (Washington, D.C.: 1975), pp. 117-118.

14. *Statistical Abstract 1992*, p. 11.

15. *Historical Statistics*, p. 14.

16. *Statistical Abstract 1992*, p. 17.

17. William A. Henry III, "Beyond the Melting Pot," *Time*, April 9, 1990, p. 28.

18. Felicity Barringer, "Census Shows Profound Change in Racial Makeup of the Nation," *The New York Times*, March 11, 1991, p. A1.

19. U.S. Census Bureau, *The Foreign-Born Population in the United States* (Washington, D.C.: 1993), pp. 149, 166.

20. Linda Chavez, *Out of the Barrio: Toward a New Politics of Hispanic Assimilation* (New York: Basic Books, 1991), p. 163.

21. Michael Kaufman, "New Socialist Realism: Emigres' Bleak Canvases," *The New York Times*, November 20, 1993, p. 25.

22. Joseph Berger, "Bienvenidos a los Suburbios," *The New York Times*, July 29, 1993, p. B1.

23. "The Numbers Game," *Time*, fall 1993, p. 14.

24. Dympna Ugwu-Oju, "Pursuit of Happiness," *The New York Times Magazine*, November 14, 1993, section 6, pp. 40, 42.

25. Lynda Richardson, "Thriving on Difference," *The New York Times*, December 28, 1993, p. B1.

26. James Walsh, "The Perils of Success," *Time*, fall 1993, p. 55.

27. Michael Novak, "How American Are You If Your Grandparents Came from Serbia in 1888?", in Sallie TeSelle, ed., *The Rediscovery of Ethnicity* (New York: Harper Colophon, 1974), p. 18.

28. Arlene B. Hirschfelder and Beverly R. Singer, eds., *Rising Voices: Writings of Young Native Americans* (New York: Charles Scribner's Sons, 1992), p. 8.

29. "Beyond the Melting Pot," *Time*, April 9, 1990, p. 31.

30. Richard Rodriguez, *Days of Obligation: An Argument with My Mexican Father* (New York: Viking, 1992), p. 168.

31. Richard Rorty, "The Unpatriotic Academy," *The New York Times*, February 13, 1994, section 5, p. 15.

32. George P. Fletcher, "Update the Pledge," *The New York Times*, December 6, 1992, section 4, p. 19.

Glossary

abolition—The freeing of slaves.

acculturation—The process whereby an individual or group takes on some characteristics of another culture.

affirmative action—Active recruitment in jobs and education of blacks and other minorities who have suffered discrimination.

alien—A foreign-born resident of a country who is not a citizen.

Americanization—Speeding up the acculturation of immigrants by encouraging the adoption of American ways and the abandonment of foreign cultures.

anti-Semitism—Hostility toward Jews.

assimilation—The process whereby an individual or group loses a separate identity by taking on the characteristics of another culture.

civil rights movement—The crusade of the 1950s and the 1960s to achieve full equality for African Americans.

cultural diversity (cultural pluralism)—A state of society in which various ethnic groups are free to observe and pass on their own traditions.

culture—The way of life of a given group of people.

discrimination—Unfair, unequal treatment of an individual or group, usually based on prejudice.

emancipation—The freeing of slaves.

emigrant—A person who leaves his or her native country.

ethnic group—A group of people who share certain traits that tend to unify them and make them feel different from others.

first-generation American—A foreign-born resident of the United States.

ghetto—Originally a special quarter of a city where Jews were forced to live; now a city neighborhood inhabited by any minority group.

melting pot—Literally, a container in which separate materials are blended; figuratively, a metaphor for the United States as a blend of different peoples.

mestizo—A person of mixed Native-American and European ancestry.

metaphor—A figure of speech in which one image or idea is used to describe another, in order to suggest a likeness.

minority—A group singled out for less than equal treatment in society.

multiculturalism—An approach to society that emphasizes Americans' cultural diversity.

nationality—Citizenship in a given nation.

nativism—Anti-immigrant feeling.

naturalization—A process whereby an alien becomes a citizen.

prejudice—Negative attitudes toward an individual or group, usually based on stereotyped thinking.

race—A large group of people sharing visible physical characteristics.

racism—The belief that one race is superior to others; actions taken based on such a belief.

second-generation American—A resident of the United States whose parents were born elsewhere.

segregation—Enforced separation of a group, often on the basis of race.

sharecropper—A farmer who, instead of paying rent to the landowner, gives him or her a share of the harvested crop.

stereotype—An oversimplified mental image of a group.

WASP—An American of white Anglo-Saxon (British) Protestant descent.

Further Reading

Ashabranner, Brent. *The New Americans: Changing Patterns in U.S. Immigration*. New York: Dodd, Mead, 1983.

Bode, Janet. *New Kids on the Block: Oral Histories of Immigrant Teens*. New York: Franklin Watts, 1989.

Fuchs, Lawrence. *The American Kaleidoscope: Race, Ethnicity, and the Civic Culture*. Hanover, N.H.: University Press of New England, 1990.

Gordon, Milton M. *Assimilation in American Life: The Role of Race, Religion, and National Origins*. New York: Oxford University Press, 1964.

Greeley, Andrew M. *Why Can't They Be Like Us?: Facts and Fallacies About Ethnic Differences and Group Conflicts in America*. New York: Institute of Human Relations Press, American Jewish Committee, 1969.

Higham, John. *Send These to Me: Immigrants in Urban America*. Baltimore, Md.: Johns Hopkins University Press, 1984.

Mann, Arthur. *The One and the Many: Reflections on the American Identity*. Chicago: University of Chicago Press, 1979.

Portes, Alejandro, and Ruben G. Rumbaut. *Immigrant America: A Portrait*. Berkeley, Calif.: University of California Press, 1990.

Reimers, David. *Still the Golden Door: The Third World Comes to America*. 2d. ed., New York: Columbia University Press, 1992.

Schlesinger, Arthur M., Jr. *The Disuniting of America*. New York: W.W. Norton, 1992.

Sowell, Thomas. *Ethnic America: A History*. New York: Basic Books, 1981.

Takaki, Ronald. *A Different Mirror: A History of Multicultural America*. Boston: Little, Brown, 1993.

Terkel, Studs. *Race: How Blacks and Whites Think and Feel About the American Obsession*. New York: The New Press, 1992.

Thernstrom, Stephan, ed. *Harvard Encyclopedia of American Ethnic Groups*. Cambridge, Mass.: Harvard University Press, 1980.

Index